OVER THE WALL

By the same author:
A Pocket with a Hole. Brewin Books

For my husband, Peter

ACKNOWLEDGEMENTS:

The line drawings are by Matthew Bullock

OVER THE WALL

A working-class girl at university in the 1950s

by

Brenda Bullock

Brewin Books

First published by
Brewin Books, Studley, Warwickshire 1998

BRANDHALL

ISBN 1 85858 112 5
A British Library Cataloguing in Publication Data
Catalogue record for this book is available from
The British Library

Typeset in New Century Schoolbook
and made and printed in Great Britain
by Heron Press, Kings Norton, Birmingham

CHAPTER ONE

Into The Unknown

At the end of September 1958, my father, sufficiently impressed by the novelty of the situation of one of his daughters going as a student to a university to take the trouble, drove me in his prized Standard Vanguard, strange metallic blue paint, sloping back and odd divided windscreen and all, to the University of Leicester. All the way there I sat stiffly in the front seat, unaccustomed to travelling in such style, only too aware as the car lurched over bumps, of the rattling of the borrowed battered suitcase on the back seat, containing my somewhat pitiful collection of clothes and a few books I'd been told by the university to buy and read before I went up for my first term. I didn't feel nervous: I felt all the terror of the condemned man on his way to the scaffold. Not for the first time in my life I was about to take a reckless leap into the unknown, with only a borrowed suitcase in my hand and a couple of pounds in my purse. I tried to look unconcerned, but in my head beat the question of how I would survive financially until my grant was paid. Would I be expected to pay for my board and lodging as soon as I got there, and, if so, how on earth would I pay? I had absolutely no idea what was expected of me. Brought up, as I was, on a Council housing estate, where I was the first, and for a long time, the only, child to go to a Grammar School, let alone to a university, 'further education' was just a phrase to me, bandied about at school, but as meaningless as a hieroglyph: how universities worked, what and how they taught, how they were organised, just what was expected of me as a student, I had not the faintest idea. I merely expected gloomily that the embarrassment and mortification that had characterised my career at grammar school, where I never wore the right uniform, never had enough money to pay my bus fare to and from school, always had the impression of being entirely out on a limb, was bound to take the same path and follow me from Birmingham to Leicester.

Of course, I'd seen the university when I'd come up for my interview a few months before, when I'd been offered my place in the French Department, but as I stepped out of the car and looked round the compact little campus, I felt distressingly like an alien setting foot on a far-flung planet, an awful long way from home. I had no idea what I was going to do in a university. After all, I'd only chosen Leicester because I'd thought it would be near enough to Birmingham for it not to be too much of a problem to raise the bus fare to get there and back, and because Derek Hogg played football for Leicester City and I'd be able to watch him play. Now, here I was, not arriving by bus at all, but by car, and Derek Hogg had, to my intense irritation, been transferred to West Bromwich Albion not long after I'd accepted my place at Leicester; all of which combined to give me the distinctly unpleasant feeling that coming to university might well turn out to be an error of epic proportions. I felt like a small boy who'd shinned up and over the wall surrounding the big house, only to find himself in a world of smart clothes, posh accents and the dread of being immediately discovered to be a gatecrasher.

Stifling my gloomy feeling that it all just served me right, I looked round the small cluster of buildings with a swelling feeling of quiet satisfaction. It was one of those cosy, provincial, so-called 'red-brick' universities, only in this case there wasn't a red brick to be seen. It had only recently changed its status from a University College, offering London University degrees, to a full university, awarding its own, and it was still a quiet, enclosed backwater, reassuringly small and low-key but still, to me at least, rather impressive.

The campus occupied the site and the buildings of what had been the Leicestershire and Rutland Lunatic Asylum and the main administration building of the university, the impressively titled Fielding-Johnson building, had been the

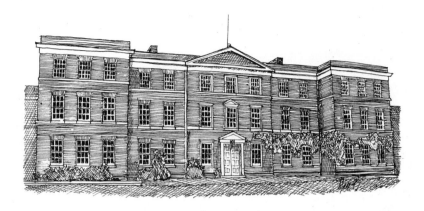

The Fielding-Johnson building

imposing facade of the old institution. It was a symmetrical, grey-stone ivy-clad building, to my mind the very embodiment of old-time academia. It dominated the campus, looking out onto a tarmaced path and rolling lawns, dotted in exam times with brightly clad knots of students, reclining on the grass, books in hand, drinking in the sunshine and the knowledge they hoped would get them through their exams. The lawns sloped down from the path to University Road in the distance, screened and muffled by the old wall that had once hemmed in the old Lunatic Asylum and by clumps of rhododendron bushes, which, come the summer, would blaze with colour, the flame-coloured blossoms, the pink, the purple and the mauve, seeming just too exotic and luxuriant for a provincial English garden.

Beside the main building sat College Hall, once the individual bedrooms of the nurses in the Asylum, now the rooms of the female students of the university. Behind this lay the hotch-potch of buildings which housed lecture rooms, just like the classrooms I had just left behind at school. The walls were painted that official cream colour, darkened by age to a dirty custard yellow, shades of post-war austerity. Rows of tables and chairs faced the lecturer's desk, just like my form-teacher's desk at school. When you saw the rooms

The Astley-Clarke building

empty it looked for all the world like a schoolroom, waiting for the children to come in from play.

On the left side of the lawn, on an angle to the main building, was the low, slate-roofed Astley-Clarke science building, the first new building on the site since the university was founded in 1921. On the other side of the lawn rose the imposing Percy Gee, Students' Union building, named after the great benefactor of the university who was named Pro-Vice Chancellor when the university gained its independence. It was a spanking new building, all bright, clean yellow brick, exuding self-confidence, and prefaced by a flight of stone steps, heralding future expansion.

This, then, was the sum total of the buildings of the university that was to be my home for three years. It really seemed to be more reminiscent of a rather exclusive boarding school than a university. In a few years, of course, the campus would become bloated as strange, alien, glass and steel structures pierced the sky, squabbling vulgarly for a place to set themselves in the restricted area of the campus, dwarfing the existing buildings as they rose ever higher, clamouring for attention. New faculties would burgeon, seemingly overnight, like mushrooms: medicine, law, engineering - and the sheer press of thousands of new

The Percy Gee building

students would soon make even the newest of buildings quickly shabby. In 1958, however, everything was on a more comforting, human scale, even the students. There were so few of them, for one thing: not much more than 800 in all - and they were clad, not in the dreary uniform of today, the blue denim and the Doc Martens, like the featureless masses of Chairman Mao's communist army, but in jumpers, sports jackets, ties, even blazers and grey flannels, like left-over school uniform. Life moved at a more sedate pace then, and it was easy to believe that I was one of the privileged 2% of young people chosen to receive the benefits of a university education.

The new dwarfing the old - The Attenborough building

CHAPTER TWO

In Hall

As I got out of the car and saw for the first time the house that was to be my home for the first year of my course, 1 Salisbury Road, I believed I'd died and gone to Heaven. It was an elegant Edwardian detached house, newly converted into a students' home. The word that came to mind was 'luxury' . For me, used to any, odd, unmatching furniture, army surplus blankets on the bed, supplemented by Dad's overcoat in very cold weather, a tiny, freezing cold bathroom with no refinements whatsoever, and having to wash, iron, shop, clean and cook for a family of five and look after the younger children, it was Paradise. I was to share a study-bedroom with Beryl, a Social Science student, a bedroom furnished with brand new pieces: desks, wardrobes, beds, all new fixtures and fittings, luxurious bathrooms and, what's more, a room-cleaning and laundry service which freed me, for the first time ever, from the drudgery of domestic chores.

1 Salisbury Road

The house was home to girls of all years and departments, the aim being to help newcomers integrate into university life with the minimum of difficulty. There were eight first-year students, including myself, from departments as varied as zoology, languages, social studies and classics, and we remained friends throughout our university careers and beyond. We were supervised by a live-in tutor, a post-graduate student, preparing her Ph.D., who tried to be strict, but whose regime was comfortably humane.

Students brought up in today's free-and-easy, do-as-you-please atmosphere would be astonished by the strictness of Hall life in those days. For one thing, Halls were strictly single-sex, and the atmosphere was just like that of an Enid Blyton school story, all girls together, peering curiously through the banisters at any man who came to call for one of the girls (and they were only allowed to advance as far as the hall), to see if he was worth looking at. We borrowed each other's clothes for special dates and spent much time chewing over our emotional lives with each other. Life was cosy and civilised.

When we came in of an evening we had to sign in on a pad on the hall table, so our tutor would know at a glance that she had a full complement before she locked the front door, which was done promptly at 11 p.m. If you intended to stop out later than this hour you had to request in advance a late key from the tutor and sign for it. Too many late keys would be bound to call forth some disapproving strictures on the lateness of your hours and a homily on the necessity for hard work and a reasonable social calendar.

Such restrictions seem a world away from today's mixed Halls of Residence, and liberated regimes, but, of course, in those days, young people didn't reach legal maturity until the age of 21, which put the university in the position of being *in loco parentis*, a duty to our parents that was taken very seriously. It certainly made a great difference to how students were viewed officially. Nowadays, with vast numbers of students, all scrambling to find a roof over their heads, have come the high tower blocks, identical, drab concrete boxes, containing small, individual, sparsely furnished cells: all the trappings of a functional philosophy. But in my day, students were seen as being sons and daughters of the university, a scarce and valuable national resource, and we were cared for and cosseted accordingly.

Not only did we have beautiful homes to live in, with all domestic services provided, but we also had all our food provided: morning and evening meal during the week and full board at weekends. All we had to do was study and pass exams: everything else was taken care of. In Salisbury Road there were no facilities for catering, so, every morning, we strolled through Victoria Park, past the impressive war memorial, decked with stone flags, draped and painted in a deceptively realistic way, past the tennis courts and the bowling greens, past the notice informing us that the greens were 'for players of either sex', which induced us, in a pathetic attempt at wit, to refer to the assembled ladies of mature years, clad in pristine white and jaunty panama hats, who generally peopled the greens, as the 'either sexes'. Turning right after the courts brought us to the Percy Gee building where we ate our breakfast with the College Hall students. In the evening we took dinner there, also, in a scene resembling an old-fashioned boarding school. On High Table sat Miss Forster, the Warden of College Hall, and acolytes and minions invited to dine on high. The rest of the room housed the students, who presented themselves for dinner with clean hands and respectable clothes. Miss Forster said Grace, then the customary bun-fight began: good old institution food - missionary stew, meat of indeterminate kind, followed by fruit pie and custard. I loved it. Cooked meals that I hadn't had to cook myself! Other students, no doubt accustomed to cuisine of a higher sort, fashionably decried Hall food, but to me, to whom a hot meal was something of a rarity, it was food of the gods.

We ate over at college during the weekend, too, except for Sunday tea, which was fetched, on a rota basis, from a central point and delivered to the individual houses. We didn't quite reach the dizzy heights of a friend of mine, who had been at Trinity, Cambridge, during the 1930s and had been served meals by dignified men in frock coats and striped trousers, but this was good enough for me. Transformation from domestic drudge to carefree student!

In my second year, the life of proverbial Riley continued, for Beryl and I moved a few doors up the road, to the house on the corner, 16 Salisbury Road, another handsome throwback to a more opulent era, where we could open our window on warm evenings and hear wafted on the summer air, the glorious strains of the "1812 Overture", bells and cannons and all, borne to us across the road from the de Montfort Hall, where a concert was in progress. Our tutor in this house was Miss Chennell, a blind spinster lady. We had had a comfortable relationship with our former tutor in our last house, but Beryl never seemed to be quite on the same wavelength as Miss Chennell, and she frequently shocked and scandalised her with unguarded remarks, which somehow seemed to slip out before she could examine their suitability for sensitive ears.

Beryl had a fetish about washing her hair, which she did at the oddest times. Many a time I came in late after an evening out, to find her kneeling, like some prostrate acolyte before a god, with her head pressed up against the

16 Salisbury Road

radiator, trying to dry her hair. One night she hit upon the wonderful plan of going to the kitchen, which we used to make drinks and snacks, and heating up the toasting implements to dry her hair. As she was heating the wire racks and holding them over her hair to dry it, Miss Chennell, attracted by the noise late at night, came into the room and enquired sociably,

"Having a late supper, dear?"

to which Beryl, who could hardly say,

"No, I'm drying my hair on the toasters,"

dutifully replied,

"Yes, Miss Chennell."

Being in one of houses separate from the university campus, if only across the park from it, and away from College Hall, helped to give us a feeling of independence from communal living. We were, of course, officially entitled to use all the facilities College Hall had to offer, the chief of these being a rather cheerless and gloomy-looking Common Room, overlooking a garden, which boasted both a record player and a radio. We were also, on odd occasions, and in strict rotation, invited, or rather summoned, to take tea with Miss Forster and make small talk about inconsequential topics that interested nobody. There were girls, much reminiscent of teacher's pets in girls' comic papers, such as "School Friend" or "Girls' Crystal", who took tea more regularly, and walked Miss Forster's dogs, but we outliers, free from the tyranny of a huge, all female environment, viewed them with disdain. When one of our first-year group actually chose to move from Salisbury Road into College Hall we could scarcely believe it, but her room-mate was glad to lose a devoutly religious girl, who read the Bible every morning from 6 a.m. onwards and seemed to disapprove of everything we did. In exchange, we gained Jill, who was sufficiently bohemian and unconventional to satisfy even the most rebellious amongst us.

The cosy, orderly and civilised life-style of the girls' Halls was, perhaps surprisingly, echoed in life at the Halls for men. Actually, until after World War Two there had been no accommodation for men on offer, but when the university Authorities decided to remedy the situation, late in the 1940s, there were no half-measures. The campus of the university, bounded as it was by Victoria Park on one side, Wyggeston Boys' School on the other, and the cemetery across the road, could not expand, so land had to be bought elsewhere. True to form, the Authorities came up trumps, buying for their Men's Halls three large mini-mansions, set in their own grounds in a very affluent area of the city, two and a half miles from the main campus. Thus, Hastings, Beaumont and Shirley Houses were purchased in the leafy suburb of Oadby, much to the fury of the residents of the opulent quarter, who in 1949 sent a petition to the Ministry of Town & Country Planning, objecting to the proposed extensions to the buildings on the site.

Surely, never can students have been housed in more beautiful and elegant surroundings, in mini stately homes, surrounded by botanical gardens of much beauty and great scientific interest. They lived in some splendour, took their meals in Beaumont House, presided over by the warden, and

Beaumont Hall

*Modern Accommodation blocks in the
grounds of Stamford Hall*

led lives every bit as orderly as the girls. They, too, had to be up and out before 9 a.m. in the morning, to give the domestic staff time to get on with their work, and they had to be home by 11 o'clock at night, just like the girls. One of the Housekeepers, Mrs Knight, was a comforting source of help and advice, just like Matron in a boarding school, and for good, solid, homespun philosophy, you couldn't beat Sylv and Anna, the two cleaners, who came in to work every day from the village of Fleckney. One day, they were deep in conversation with a student, who had commented, with some surprise, how human and friendly the house tutor was. Sylv gave the matter some thought and then opined, "Ay, m'duck, but they all do it in the same po, don't they?"

which seems to me to be a fair summing up of human equality in the sight of God!

However, this very belief in equality was bound, sooner or later, to force changes. All too soon Halls of Residence would be mixed-sex, with few or no rules, come and go as you please, self-catering, functional blocks of rooms in the grounds of the stately houses, encroaching on the previously spacious grounds, and College Hall demolished to make way for the new library, while a new, purpose-built College Hall was built on a site away from the campus. Days of leisure to study, without being burdened with domestic chores were over, and we were dragged, willing or not, into the real world.

CHAPTER THREE

Undergraduate Life

Coming as I did from a working-class background, from a large Council housing estate, I had no idea what 'further education' meant in practice: to me it was just a phrase bandied about at school. So, when I suddenly found myself deposited, all alone, at university, my first feeling was one of blind panic. For a whole week, the traditional 'freshers' week', which was designed to introduce us to university life and persuade us to join any number of clubs that were on offer to us, I reeled about from place to place in something of a daze. In an era when only one working class girl in five hundred went to a university, I felt horribly conspicuous. We were still in an age when a university education was almost exclusively the preserve of the middle and upper classes, and these classes of students were well used to the refinements of life that left me pop-eyed with amazement. We were just beginning to see a glimmer of change: although the vast majority of the girls were resolutely middle class, with names like Celia and Angela, there had already begun a drive to attract working class boys into higher education and the university was beginning to fill up with lads, many of them from the East End of London, who had reassuringly ordinary names like Dave, Sid and Ray, and accents to match. To me, however, somewhat out on a limb, it was all horribly foreign, and for a while I found it hard to settle. What floored me more than anything was the strange artificiality of a society where everybody was much the same age and doing much the same thing. It was to be more than twenty years before large numbers of mature students were to be welcomed into universities, to widen the age range and add a new dimension, and I found the hot-house atmosphere of hundreds of people, all the same age, all doing the same thing, totally stifling.

To help me keep a more normal perspective on life, in those

early days I took to going down town, to the open market, and watching ordinary people of every age going about the normal business of everyday living, a welcome reassurance to me that ordinary, normal human life was still going on while I was 'away at university'. I really found there was something about the open market that was uplifting to the spirits. Early in the morning you had the smell of fresh fruit: polished apples you could see your face in; huge hands of yellow and green bananas; prickly pineapples, their hand-grenade appearance hiding the delicious sweetness that lurked within. Then there was the noise: the incessant tramp of feet, the noise that just the bustle of people creates; the encouraging patter of the stall-holders, the flamboyant oratory of the man on the crockery stall, promising, with all the zeal of a hell-fire preacher, huge amounts of fancy crockery "Not for £5, not even for £4, but for a measly thirty bob!"

How could anyone resist! Then there were the textures: shiny smooth apples, crinkly melons, the soft sensuality of slippery satin nightdresses, daringly low cut, with all the promise of heavenly nights.

Yes, of course, by the afternoon it would all be the pervading stench of rotting vegetables, feet kicking up litter, slimy green streaks on the pavement where unwary people had slipped on discarded cabbage stalks; bored stall-holders, more interested in a reviving cup of tea than a late customer. But I loved it and it always raised my spirits enough, with its sheer energy and life, to go back and get on with the academic life.

Slowly, of course, I got used to things. I got used to having, for the first and only time in my life, a bank account. Back home, nobody I knew had any more money than what they had in their pocket. But I had a full grant, enough money to see me through the whole term, with just enough left over to pay my bus fare back to Birmingham and see me delivered, penniless, back home, to get through the vacation as best I could. Every week in term time I made the journey to the bank to take out £2 to pay my expenses for the week, for lunches, coffee and entertainment. Actually, I drew out only £1.19s 11d, since the bank clerk, horrified at my having to pay 2d stamp duty every time I drew out £2 or more, always insisted I drew out less than £2 and cheated the bank out of a precious 2d. To me, to have such a large sum of money; me, who was used to having to walk miles to save 1d in bus fare, was an occasion for rejoicing, but I was not used to extravagance and my money lasted the week well enough.

Even paying for entertainment didn't make too much of a hole in the finances, for social life tended to centre on the Students' Union building, and there were plenty of activities on offer. The year before I went up to Leicester there had been no union building and all social occasions had had to take place in a variety of hired rooms dotted across the city, but we had a handsome new building, with facilities to match. Life centred around the coffee bar: through the main doors, down the stairs and there it was on your left. Here chaos reigned. At coffee times it was always the same: two queues of daunting length trickled slowly to the counter, where harassed women, in overalls of sickly green, dispensed a liquid of suspiciously indeterminate colour into thick melamine cups, stained with the evidence of former brews. Around the room squatted islands of small tables, rickety and with scuffed tops, almost foundering beneath their cargo of used cups and the masses of students who clustered round them, like drowning men clinging to a raft, leaning over precariously in their plastic chairs, that squeaked protestingly as they moved, to deposit their cup and saucer in any available square inch of space on the already overburdened table top. The queues meandered their leisurely way in a haphazard fashion between the tables, snaking out almost as far as the door, impeding the passage of the clumps of jostling students, all trying to juggle books, bags, coffee cups and plates of frosty-looking iced buns, as they gingerly picked their way through the crowds to an empty seat.

At some time during the day you were sure to see everybody you knew in the coffee bar and even at weekends it was just as busy. On Saturday night it was usually taken over by the brawny rugby types, who assaulted the unwilling ears of the uninitiated with the time-honoured, if tedious, rugby songs, which generally drove the uncommitted to seek sanctuary elsewhere, in the Junior Common Room upstairs.

Naturally, the staff did not take coffee in the melee of the students' coffee bar, but in the more quiet and reflective atmosphere of the Senior Common Room. In years to come, when the Charles Wilson building had sprung up, beanstalk like, opposite the Percy Gee, the staff had a Common Room high up in the building, with picture windows that offered a panoramic view of the fast expanding campus. This room formed an oasis in a desert of stir, a place of carpeted silence, deep upholstered chairs and an atmosphere totally different from the scuffed scruffiness of the students' coffee bar, with its plastic chairs and seething masses.

Entertainment came in many forms, all of them affordable. Apart from all the societies, where you could try everything from acting in a variety of dramatic productions, to lively debates, mountain climbing or local history, a whole range of pastimes that ranged from the energetic to the eccentric, there was the film society where, for only a shilling a time, you could see a whole season of good films. Saturday night found the energetic at the weekly hop, where you could try out your natty new dance steps, cutting a swathe through the unwary, hurling yourself into the jive, while the unadventurous stuck to the strict tempo of waltz, quick-step and fox-trot.

For someone like me, whose total social life before I came to university had consisted of visits to the cinema and swimming on Sunday mornings, this was a revelation. There was so much to do and, to my astonishment, there were always many young men wishing to accompany me. I suddenly found myself in the delicious situation of being found attractive by the opposite sex, and I revelled in the new-found attention. However, the famous "swinging sixties" hadn't yet burst upon a startled world, bringing, thanks to the miraculous "pill", a sexual revolution, and, generally speaking, relations between the sexes were not a great deal more liberated than they had been when I was at school, where obsessive and frenzied interest in the subject of sex had not been matched by a corresponding wealth of experience. At university it wasn't really all that different, even though, of course, there were those whose sexual adventures were the stuff of legends, to be recounted and tutted over enviously by the rest of us. There were the familiar tales of certain girls leaping from one man's bed to that of his friend, and one student of prodigious sexual appetite managed to get a Swedish exchange student pregnant, which gave us all the entertaining spectacle of her avenging parent appearing, demanding vengeance and retribution, but, generally, there was precious little opportunity for most people to enjoy a breathlessly exciting sex life. Apart from the very real threat of an unwanted pregnancy, there was also the fact that the Halls of Residence were strictly single-sex, so there was nowhere to take a paramour. Men were only allowed into the hall of the girls' residences, to collect a girl for a date, and so, unless you were old enough to have a rented flat (and students were not allowed to rent flats until they were 21), then privacy of the sort required to conduct steamy love affairs just wasn't available.

There were those who tried, with varying degrees of success, to subvert the system, but generally authority won. I suppose this was because if a university was to attract the well-bred daughters of the middle classes out of the shelter of their parents' care, then parents had to be assured that their daughters would be as safe there as at home, so rules were rigidly enforced. Not that this stopped the usual silly, undergraduate pranks, such as the night some unfortunate lad (now a respectable diplomat!) was trussed up by his

fellows and deposited at dead of night in the hallway of the
Hall of Residence of the girls from the Domestic Science
College, where he was discovered , wearing little else than
an embarrassed smile, early next morning by the startled
warden of the home. But, to our regret, we just missed out
on the era of the sexual revolution: ours was a more innocent
age, where only the most outrageous were willing to kick
their hat so far over the windmill as never to see it again.

But, of course, no age is immune to personal tragedies, and
our department had one of the most distressing. In our first
year we were only twenty students (6 boys and 14 girls -
languages in those days were deemed to be a 'girls' subject'
which not many boys studied). During the vacation after the
first year, Jill, arguably the most talented of any of us girls,
went off to France, met a man and returned to England
pregnant. She was offered the chance to take the next year
off to have her child and then resume her university course
the year after, but the father was so keen to marry Jill and
have the child that she felt it was her duty to do this. Thus,
they married and went to Algeria, where his parents lived.
At this time, Algeria was in the middle of the terrorist
troubles with the OAS and violence was common. One day
Jill and her husband, fleeing from a terrorist attack, crashed
their car. Jill was seriously injured and the child was born
prematurely and dead. After this tragedy, the marriage,
begun on such shaky foundation, struggled on for a while
and ultimately foundered, leaving Jill, penniless, with no
qualifications and with a young daughter to support. The
girl with the glittering academic career in front of her, thus
found herself alone, to sink into depression and poverty.

In view of this story, which ought to have offered a salutary
lesson to us all, I was intensely astonished to find that there
were girls who came up to university, not to gain a valuable
education, but with the express intention of finding a
husband whose education would promise future economic
success. More than a few came up just to hunt a mate and,
having achieved that objective, promptly failed their exams

and were sent down, to wait for their fiances to graduate and keep them in the manner to which they intended to become accustomed.

Looking back, I'm amazed to find what an amount of shared projects we all got involved in. Rag week, when money was raised for charity, usually got everybody roped in, in one capacity or another, in an attempt to persuade the long-suffering citizens of Leicester to part with their cash for good causes. Floats were designed and made for the procession, illustrating the theme for the year. In my first year, the theme was -AGE, which gave rise to a float with a jazz band, illustrating band-AGE and other such ingenious workings of the theme. For my contribution, I intended, with a couple of friends, to borrow some university scarves (which most students sported in those days), and sew them together to make skimpy dresses to be worn as we collected money from people watching the procession. As the picture (page 22) shows, however, the weather that day was uncompromisingly vile and we were forced out of sheer self-preservation to wear jumpers and tights as well, to keep out the cold.

The culminating act of Rag Week was the Rag Revue, a theatrical extravaganza where I made my first (and last) stage appearance as a Victorian mother in a sketch of excruciating corniness. The show took place, appropriately enough, in the old Corn Exchange in town, where the future actors and television producers came up with a show, full of all the worn-out old jokes one expects from undergraduates, to whit:

"That can't be right! Have your eyes ever been checked?"
"No, they've always been blue."
or:
"Dear Sir,
Since taking your product I am a changed man.
(signed) Mrs Ivy Gribble

At least they got a laugh in those far-off days!

Rag Day 1959

The finale of the show was a spoof of the popular television pop show, "Drumbeat", rechristened "Crumbeat" and starring a suitably moody and magnificent replica of the latest star in the pop firmament, Cliff Richard.

But life wasn't all one heady round of social pleasure; we had lectures to attend, books to read, essays to write. In those simple days we didn't have 'seminars', 'workshops' or 'brain-storming sessions', just 'lectures' or 'tutorials'; we didn't complete 'assignments', we wrote 'essays'. Attendance at lectures was compulsory and we had to sign in at each lecture to verify our attendance. For all official business, such as lectures, tutorials or visits to staff we were expected to wear undergraduate gowns: short, knee-length black academic gowns, which we tended to obtain in an emergency by going into the nearest cloakroom, removing the gown on the nearest peg and borrowing that, returning it after use. We not only addressed staff in a formal way - Mr This or Professor That, but we were addressed by them with the same formality. Today's egalitarian and ubiquitous use of first names between staff and students was many years away.

Students who did a special subject (mine was French), had to study for five terms a subsidiary subject. I chose English and thus found myself a member of the English department, presided over by the genial Professor Humphreys, one of those rare people who looked even better close to than from a distance. Professor Humphreys' philosophy was simple: students could read (and be guaranteed a question on in the exam) any author of the chosen period they wished to read, which took a lot of worry out of revising for exams. At the beginning of the course I was rather taken aback, not to mention offended, to be given a course of lectures by Professor Humphreys, devoted to such things as grammar, letter-writing and the like. In these days of falling student literacy there may be some point to it, but then I felt distinctly miffed that it was thought necessary to offer such elementary instruction to students who had chosen to do

English at university.

We were allocated a tutor for the year, for whom we wrote our fortnightly essays, and I found myself assigned to Dr Fraser. George Fraser, a rather unsavoury-looking character in a crumpled suit, was the friend of poets such as T.S. Eliot, and a well-known poet in his own right, a fact that caused us no little embarrassment. One day, unknown to us, he slipped one of his poems into our literary criticism class and invited comments on it. We all said most unflattering things about it: no-one seemed to like it, and one girl asserted she wouldn't read it for pleasure. When he admitted, with some reluctance, after we asked who the author was,

"Well, actually, it's one of mine."

the classroom emptied as if by magic!

There were three of us assigned to Dr Fraser, and we had our tutorials with him in his study, one of the minute cells that had once done service in the old Lunatic Asylum. It was so tiny that to get four people in there, with chairs and a desk, meant that they all had to be either very good friends or built like stickmen. We had to jam our chairs up against the door, while Dr Fraser sat at the desk. If someone came inopportunely to the door, during a tutorial and opened it unexpectedly we would be spilled embarrassingly into his lap, thus reducing the serious business of our literary gems to farce. It was bad enough already, for he had the disconcerting habit of reading our work out loud to us, with all the pauses in the wrong places, thus reducing our pearls of wisdom to nonsense.

"It is evident that Claudio was bent .... on marrying her," he would intone solemnly, in his flat Scottish burr, while we hid our giggles as best we could.

Being only subsiduary students we tended to have mostly one lecturer, the energetic Miss Jones. From a distance, Monica Jones looked like one of the students: tight sweater, straight skirt, stockings of fancy colours and patterns, and stiletto-heeled shoes. On getting closer, however, you would see she was too old to be a student, even though she bounced along with the spring in the step one associates with the young. She swept into lectures a few minutes after 9 o'clock, breathless and carrying a basket full of shopping, then launched into her lecture like a mini tornado. She always read her lectures, rather than speaking just from short notes, and it was obvious that she marked out before each lecture just how many pages she had to get through, for if she started late, she speeded up her delivery as the lecture progressed , so that we had to take notes faster and faster in an effort to keep up. She seemed to be the maid of all work in the department, lecturing to us on many different authors and periods. What we didn't know and what would have caused no little amazement and prurient interest had we known it, was that Miss Jones, so unremarkable in so many ways, was deeply embroiled at that time in an ultimately tragic love affair with the poet Philip Larkin, who had been a librarian at Leicester before my arrival. Had we known what anguish she was to suffer in later years, when she was finally abandoned by the man she'd stuck faithfully to for years, we might well have seen her in a new and more sympathetic light.

Most lecturers, however, were fairly unremarkable as people, whatever their lecturing skills. The days of the old-fashioned, absent-minded, eccentric professor, had gone, consigned to history or myth. Or nearly. There was still Professor Leon, head of the Classics Department. He was legend writ large. He was an untidy, shuffling figure, who wore his rag-bag clothes like a bundle of rubbish done up ugly. His head was topped by a shock of wild white hair and on his feet he favoured crepe-soled sandals worn without socks, in which he squeaked and squelched up and down the rows of desks when he was invigilating exams, disturbing the silence of the exam room with his noisy progress. It was rumoured that another professor, coming upon him during a walk in the country, when hailed by him, had taken him for a tramp and threatened to set his dog on him, which, given his odd appearance, one could well believe. He rode his bicycle, bicycle clips and all, so slowly that sometimes, with his mind obviously on other things, he forgot to pedal at all and promptly fell off, spilling himself inelegantly and dangerously into the middle of the road.

He was every bit as absent-minded as professors are, by repute, meant to be. He never recognised his students, even when they came to see him at his request, which led to much criticism: students took offence at being totally invisible to their professor. One day, when a member of staff was talking to him about a man the Professor swore he didn't know, the other man, exasperated, snapped:

"Good heavens, man! He's a member of your department, you must know him!"

to which Professor Leon crowed triumphantly:

"Well, there you are, then! How do you expect me to know my own students if I don't even know my own staff!"

Point made, he retreated again into his own little world.

But he was just an anachronism, a dinosaur fossil that proved they had once existed. In the French Department things were done differently.

CHAPTER FOUR

The French Department

I chose to study French only after a lot of thought. I'd always been good at French: at school I'd taken to the subject like the proverbial duck to water, partly because I'd had such an excellent teacher at school, the ferocious Mr Mills, who would countenance no slacking or half-heartedness. Failure to get at least 17 out of 20 for the regular vocabulary tests would inevitably mean detention, which tended to concentrate the mind of even the most desultory student wonderfully well! When I came up to Leicester for interview, to be grilled by the equally ferocious Professor Sykes, I startled him somewhat half way through my interview by blurting out, "I'm not sure that I don't want to do English instead," and was promptly despatched to see Professor Humphreys, who duly offered me a place in his department. Somehow, on my way back to Professor Sykes' study I made up my mind to do French after all, (I still don't know what made me decide that), but I've never had any reason to regret my choice of department.

The French Department then was intentionally small and rigorously selective: 'elitist' to use the jargon of today. In each of the years of the special degree course only twenty students were accepted, a legacy of the old university's intention to keep student numbers manageably small. Certainly the numbers were smaller than those in many other departments even then, which was both a blessing and a curse for the students. On the plus side, we had very much personal, individual attention and felt that we were both known and valued as members of the department, but on the minus side, any misdemeanours were immediately horribly visible. You couldn't get a friend to sign in for you if you wanted to miss a lecture - all lecturers could count to twenty and your absence would be easily discovered! You couldn't miss pieces of set work: Professor Sykes kept an inventory of each piece of work set for each student, and to miss one would lead to a summons to account for yourself and your unacceptable sloth. Sometimes we got the makings of a persecution complex when we had the spooky feeling that our every move was being watched.

The chief detector of all breaches of duty was Professor Sykes. Leslie Sykes was what these days is dismissively referred to as "a man of the old school". He believed in the old-fashioned values of hard work, academic rigour and the value of experience over youth, all of which, in this age of the worship of youth, wouldn't go down very well. These days it is looked upon as a virtue that students help choose what they study and rejoice at having lecturers of their own generation 'to whom they can really relate'. In my day, lecturers who had most experience, most maturity, were most valued, but, all too soon, professors who told students what they would study and how it was to be done would become *persona non grata*, even in their own departments, treated like dinosaurs and rapidly rendered extinct.

Professor Sykes would accept nothing flabby or that smacked of woolly thinking. Over the three years of our course we studied an amazing amount of things. We did the history of the French language from Latin to Modern French, medieval literature, linguistics. We studied the novel, theatre, poetry and philosophy from the sixteenth century onwards, we did translations from French into English and English into French, essays in French, oral French, practical literary criticism, French history, geography and Modern Institutions and culture, all of which kept us pretty busy, (on the principle, I suppose, that the Devil makes work for idle hands!) We were examined not only at the end of the year but at the end of each term, tortures which were followed by the mortifying experience of an interview with Professor Sykes, where we were told, in no uncertain terms, of our inevitable shortcomings!

The department was arranged differently from the English department, where we had a single tutor who marked all our essays on every author. In the French department we wrote essays for the expert in that subject and then had to suffer a half-hour, one-to-one tutorial where we had to defend what we had written to the person who knew most on that subject. In Professor Sykes' tutorials I frequently felt that execution would be kinder than that torture, but Dr Hampton, who struggled manfully for two years to try to make me appreciate philosophy, could always be relied upon to show the gentle kindness of a favourite uncle and let me off far more lightly than I knew my total ineptitude deserved.

If it all sounds like mental torture - it was! But it was the most wonderful intellectual training anyone could get and one for which I have had reason to be grateful all my life. Sharp, incisive thinking, intellectual rigour and an unwillingness to accept anything illogical or woolly has given me the ability to cope with the most difficult intellectual task and an unwillingness to accept less from others. It may well be difficult to live with, but it was equally hellishly difficult to acquire, and summed up for me what a university is all about: to teach good brains to function better.

The Class of 1962

We were also lucky in that our department was primarily a teaching department. In some departments, staff look upon students as something of a nuisance, who interrupt their research and take up too much time in lectures, essay marking and the like, but in our department we never went over to college for lectures only to find a notice on the board proclaiming "Dr So-and-So will not lecture today". If a lot was expected of the students, just as much was expected of the staff, including the Professor. Indeed, the older he got, the more lecturing Professor Sykes seemed to do. He used to complain that he was doing more teaching than he had when a young lecturer, and we were the gainers. I, in particular, gained immeasurably from this atmosphere. All my life I'd had a home life that was at best unhappy and at worst awful, with people I couldn't look up to or aspire to emulate. Now I had people whom I could respect, who knew a great deal about a lot of things and who, what's more, were only too pleased to share their knowledge with me. I don't pretend to have been a model student: I was not only depressingly ignorant about most things but was both lacking in confidence and much given to sloth, but even I had to learn something when so much was offered me. These days, people turn up their noses at such programmes of study, laid out by staff, without consultation with the students, but how can ignorant youngsters have any inkling of how much worthwhile stuff there is to study? And, anyway, even in the late 1950s we were studying not only the great classics of the past but also new movements in art and literature, learning about the dadaists and the theatre of the absurd, studying plays that had only recently been written.

Of course, life wasn't just about earnest students, paragons of virtue and industry, falling gratefully upon the pearls of wisdom that fell from the lips of god-like teachers, sitting, so to speak, at the feet of Sophocles, drinking in his wisdom. After all, the very clever are all too prone to be eccentric or plain batty, so we had plenty of lighter moments to entertain us.

We had Dr Matthews, for a start. John Matthews, a brilliant and precocious scholar, who also had the distinct, if totally unfair, advantage of being devastatingly handsome, in an Errol Flynn type way, was the bane of the mentally slow or self-righteous. If you deserved it, you would be guaranteed to feel the rapier edge of his tongue. He once wrote on one of my essays, "You are not excused the use of the acute accent until French gives it up," and in the lecture room there was always an edge to the atmosphere, while we waited to see just who would be the butt of his sharp-tongued wit. Personally, he was entirely without vanity and had an engaging line in self-deprecation and wry humour, but he didn't suffer fools gladly. One day, when he was giving back work to us, he dropped a piece of paper on the floor. He bent down to retrieve it while the girl sitting at the table, afraid of attracting his attention, looked studiously the other way. For what seemed an age he ferreted about on the floor, while the student modestly averted her gaze. Finally, she felt a tap on the knee and as she looked down he flashed her an ironic smile, saying,

"Let's compromise, shall we? You take your foot off it and I'll pick it up!"

and one day, receiving a French prose on a scruffy, dog-eared piece of paper, he gave a look of ironic sympathy and enquired,

"Grant run out already, Mr Feinson?"

Classes with Dr Harris were even more fun. Roy Harris taught history of the French language and linguistics, dull-sounding subjects which with him were anything but dull. He was a small, impish figure, who livened up lectures with comments that ranged from the amusing to the plain daft. Once, when explaining that we don't learn much about the language from Roman gravestones, he waved airly and said,

"You don't get anything more than 'Here lies the body of Julius Bloggs,

Who died with his boots on, fighting the wags'"

He had a fund of racy stories to illustrate his rather esoteric subject, which prompted Janet, who was rather prim, to denounce him as being 'disgusting', but I thought he was wonderful. One day, when I was sitting in his study, discussing with him an essay I'd written for him, he was sitting opposite me across the desk, a diminutive figure, balancing his chair dangerously on the back legs as he put his feet on the desk, as he expounded, with much arm-waving, his opinions on the poet Villon. We were just in the middle of what I hoped was a learned discussion on the subject when suddenly there was a mighty crash and with a strangled cry he disappeared from view behind the desk. For some seconds I waited for him to reappear or at least make some sound, but there was only silence. Thinking it was prudent to at least have a look, in case he'd broken his neck or knocked himself out, I got up and peered nervously over the desk, to find him sitting wedged in the wastepaper basket, red-faced, in fits of suppressed laughter. I offered a helping tug to release him from the bin, then, Villon forgotten, went on my way.

All too soon, however, terms came to an end and I used my last shillings to buy a bus ticket back to Birmingham for the vacation, back to a different world. When I got home I slipped back into the family with scarcely a word from anyone. I either evicted whichever sister had taken possession of my bed in my absence or just got in with whoever was in possession. Mom breathed a sigh of relief because I was back to look after the girls and take over the chores of running the house and staving off disaster, while she went out to work and left me to it. For the next four weeks I would slip back into my old role, which I had been doing ever since I was twelve: shopping, cooking, cleaning, child-minding, until it was time for me to return to Leicester and leave the family to sink back into its usual state of chaos. No-one asked how I was doing at college or what I did when I was away from home, so I said nothing about it. When I'd first gone up to university, in a fit of amiability I had invited Mom and my Gran to come up to Leicester to see the place where I was studying, to give them some idea of my new life. Sadly, it had been an unqualified disaster. They were totally bewildered by it all and intimidated by everything. Gran was afraid to go into any of the official buildings in case she wasn't allowed there and someone came to evict her, and they wandered about the campus in a state bordering on alarm, unable to settle or take in anything they saw. They stood about, dressed in their best clothes, like tailor's dummies that someone had taken out of the shop window and forgotten to put back, and it was with a palpable feeling of relief that they boarded the bus after tea to go back to the familiar surroundings of home.

A lot has been said and written over the years about the problems of working-class children who get a university education, which cuts them off from their working-class roots and their families. Writers have been at pains to show how awkward it is for both child and family when the child returns, to find the family the same but himself irrevocably changed. In my case, however, the rift had grown long before I went away. I had always stuck out like the proverbial sore thumb; I hated the mood of acceptance that I saw in the people on the housing estate where I lived - acceptance of their narrow, circumscribed lives, and a total lack of ambition to look further than the traditional lot of the working classes. The boys accepted a future consisting of a job in a factory, working long hours, then early marriage to a local girl, followed by the daily grind of providing for a wife and family, with only the pub and football at weekends to lighten the burden. The girls saw no more to life than a couple of years working in a factory, or at best a shop, before marriage, children and the eternal problem of how to make ends meet. That way of life depressed me and inevitably meant a separation from both family and neighbourhood. To the neighbours, university was a concept they didn't understand; they used to ask my mother,

"How's your Bren getting on at school?"

giving a disapproving sniff as they said it, to show what they thought of children who needed to be at school at 21, instead of being in work and bringing a wage into the house.

But my longing to escape meant a huge leap into the unknown. Just as I had once been the only child on the estate to go to a grammar school, so I found myself just as alien at university. If I didn't fit in at home, neither did I find myself wholly at home with my friends at university, who had had very different experiences from mine. They had decent clothes, a life that didn't mean counting every penny, loving and affluent parents. I had not. I, whose home life had been at best grim, couldn't wait to exchange it for something better; anything better. They were at home both at university and in their home environment. I belonged nowhere, but had only a longing to spread my wings and shake off, if I could, the baggage of deprivation, even if the world I moved to was in many ways just as foreign as the world I had left behind.

But, of course, it wasn't like this for all working class students. During my first year at university I used sometimes to sit in English lectures next to a lad who seemed to me to be comfortingly familiar: narrow trousers, fashionable hair-cut, the toned-down Teddy Boy gear of the 1950s working-class boy. After the first year, however, he disappeared, dropping out because he feared the different values and ethos of university life would destroy his working class culture and drive a wedge between him and his family, cutting him off from his roots. His name was Ray Gosling, and he went on to become a famous writer and broadcaster, looking with humour and insight into people and places of all sorts. His imaginative quirkiness, his original view of life, came from his roots, and he was right to preserve them. Perhaps, after all, it's more to do with happy, secure homes, and unhappy ones, not to do with working or middle-class homes. Certainly, what worked for Ray wouldn't have worked for me. I had to get away to re-invent myself: Ray had to stay to develop what he had.

Of course, however, when I went back home during the vacations I fitted seemlessly into the fabric of life at home, trying to keep our heads above water, keeping the household ticking over, seeing that the younger children were fed, the house cleaned and Dad's dinner was on the table when he came in from work, scrounging half a crown whenever I could from my Gran or my brother, who was working, to go into town for a welcome trip out in an evening. My essays couldn't be done during the day; I had too much else to do, so, after an evening out I regularly sat up at night until the early hours of the morning, crouching by the dying embers of the fire, reading books and writing essays.

Back in Leicester, the end of the second year brought a great change. We'd been accepted on the course only on the understanding that we agreed to spend our third year in France, to perfect our spoken language and further our education, before returning to complete our degree. As the end of the second year approached, we duly wrote off applications to find ourselves jobs as language assistants in French schools. The assistant scheme was a reciprocal arrangement between the English and the French governments, whereby we took their language students into our schools, to teach oral French to our pupils, and we were welcomed into their schools on the same basis. In fact, the French assistants we had had in my school had been the only native speakers of the language I had ever heard. We were all interviewed, expressed a preference for the part of France we would like to be sent to, and, in due course, were accepted as ambassadors for our country abroad, a task that we were encouraged to take seriously. We all found places, in towns as far scattered as Nice, Laval, Bordeaux, and prepared to do our bit for Anglo-French relations. I was, as I had requested, to spend my year in Brittany, in St Brieuc, a town on the north coast.

The only fly in the ointment, as usual, was how I was going to find enough money to pay my train fare to Southampton, my ferry fare to St Malo and then my train fare to St Brieuc.

The answer was, I had to find a job. I found work for the summer in a branch of the grocery chain, Maypole Dairies, a small shop on the Coventry Road in Small Heath, Birmingham. Here I worked for the whole of the summer vacation, working five and a half days a week for the vast sum of £5 a week. I cut and weighed bacon, cheese, butter and lard, served cooked meats, eggs and a multitude of packets and tins, ate a frugal lunch in the tiny back room behind the shop, was frequently bitten and scratched by the shop cat, who appeared to be severely psychotic, and managed to save precious little of my weekly £5, after paying for bus-fares and lunches.

One thing I did discover while I was there was why shop assistants are by reputation so surly and unhelpful. Exposure to customers who get you to weigh out odd amounts of butter, or several rashers of bacon, only to decide after all the work is done that they don't want it after all, or the sadistic few who arrive regularly just as you are about to close after a long day, and beg to be admitted on the plea that

"I only want one thing"

and then stay at least fifteen minutes after closing time, stocking up with enough provisions to withstand a three-month siege, is enough to try the patience and goodwill of even the most easy-going and reduce even the saintly to ungodly cursing.

Finally, at the end of September, I left the grocery store and prepared to take yet another leap into the unknown. I'd never been to France. I'd never been able to afford to go on the regular exchange visits arranged by my school, my spoken French was rather suspect, and I had absolutely no idea what to expect. However, thanks to an emergency loan of £11 from my father, my passage was booked and I was despatched to make my own way to Southampton and on to yet another adventure.

CHAPTER FIVE

Off To France - Brittany

In 1960, when I went to Brittany, it was nothing like the
tourist playground and economic boom area that it is today.
Indeed, foreigners were few and far between: in my whole
year in St Brieuc I only met two British tourists. There were,
of course, resorts, but these catered mostly for French
holidaymakers. First there was Dinard, on the north coast,
which had been a fashionable resort of the English in
Edwardian days and still had the wide curve of the fine
sandy beach, the little casino and the street named after the
English King George V as reminders of a more chic past.
Then there was La Baule, on the Atlantic coast, which was
the playground of the smart set, offering water sports of all
kinds, but, generally, Brittany was a well-kept secret, known
only to the affluent Parisians who owned villas in the little
hidden bays, to which they escaped in the heat of a Paris
summer.

In 1960 there was no fine network of roads, no economic
miracle that saw the growth of successful food-processing

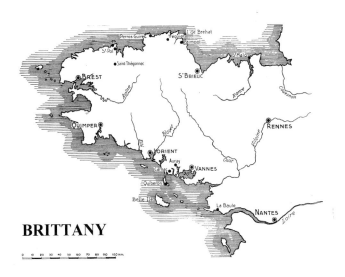

BRITTANY

industries. Brittany was a forgotten backwater, an almost foreign province, Celtic and Breton speaking, so far from the Central Government in Paris as to be entirely ignored by officialdom. Many Bretons eked out a precarious living, growing early vegetables that all too often they couldn't sell at a profit, hence the demonstrations that saw the streets of St Pol de Léon filled with artichokes, dumped by disgruntled farmers who couldn't get a decent price for them, and the protests that took the farmers to Paris, to sell their potatoes on the streets of the capital for twopence a kilo.

Apart from farming, all Brittany could offer was the sea. Surrounded as it is on three sides by the sea, it was a land of seafarers. In the days of old, the piratical Corsairs had their stronghold in St Malo, a walled and fortified town on the sea, from which they preyed on passing shipping, taking their booty back with them behind the strong walls of their town. In World War Two, the whole city was destroyed by bombing by the Canadian Air Force, but was completely rebuilt as it had been after the war, at Canadian expense. In 1960 many young men still found a living on the sea, either sporting the round blue cap with red pom-poms of the French navy, stationed at the big naval base at Brest, or as

Old Breton ladies Spinning

fishermen, sailing out of ports such as Paimpol to travel to the far fishing grounds of Icelandic waters, wresting a living from the sea itself.

The land of Brittany was wild, with a rocky, craggy coastline and a rugged interior, whose native plants were the prickly yellow gorse and the purple moorland heather. The Atlantic coast was buffeted by wild seas, where you could lean over the harbour wall and watch the powerful waves surging over the jagged rocks beneath, seething and hissing like an angry dragon as they retreated and smiting the rocks with enough force to pulverise them to the finest sand. "Worse things happen at sea", so they say, and watching this ferocious battle between land and sea, one can easily believe it. The Pointe du Raz is the most westerly point of Europe, sticking out into the sea, a finger pointing the way to America, many miles across the wild Atlantic Ocean. On the North coast the sea is gentler. Dinard is set on the Emerald Coast, that area where the sea really is an opalescent green colour, like a semi-precious stone, and further along the coast is the Coast of Pink Granite, whose pink cliffs rise from the sea, weathered by wind and water into fantastic, grotesque shapes, like Henry Moore statues.

To me Brittany was a mirror-image of Cornwall: the same rugged coast, same picturesque bays, same harsh rocky interior, same shared Celtic culture and same rural poverty. There is even an area of Brittany called Cornwall (la Cornouaille) and the ancient legends of King Arthur and the Knights of the Round Table, take place not only in Tintagel in Cornwall, but also in locations in Brittany. In fact many of the towns in Brittany were founded by Celtic saints, who came over the sea from Ireland, Cornwall and Wales to found the cities that still bear their names: St Brieuc, St Jacut, St Guirec.

As you move inland from the coast, the rocky bays with their fine sand, give way to the rocky, barren interior, the granite moorland that reminds you of Dartmoor. The coastland, called Armor in Breton is replaced by the interior, called Argoat and it is bleak, rocky and poor. In 1960 it was remote and wild, with squat little granite houses that crouched near to the earth as if stubbornly refusing to give up the struggle against parsimonious nature. This was a land where Breton was spoken more than French and where the inhabitants saw themselves as Breton first and French only second. They were a Celtic people, closer to the Welsh and the Cornish than to the French and the little roadside granite calvaries you saw at the side of small country roads reminded you of their primitive ancient faith that aligned them with the Celtic peoples of Europe. The interior was shrouded, mysterious, a land of myth and legend, where you got the impression that it still dwelt in the Middle Ages rather than in the twentieth century. There were small villages, like St Thégonnec and Guimilliau, which boasted beautiful calvaries, masterpieces of medieval art, with the most intricate carving, telling the Biblical stories of the Saints in stone, housed in sleepy little villages where tourists hardly ever ventured.

There were dense ancient forests, in whose centre could be found the hut of the sabot maker, still plying his art of hollowing out wood to make the wooden shoes that were still

Calvary at Guimilliau

worn on rural farms. It was like stepping back in time, to a time when history was still mixed with legend. The statue of St Guirec, on the beach at Ploumanach, still had nubile girls coming to it to prick the nose of the saint with a pin, hoping that he would send them a husband soon, and legend had it that the cathedral at Tréguier had once had a wooden statue of its patron saint, St Jean, which had been burnt by jealous clergy, because they feared their congregation was worshipping the statue rather than Christ. All that now remains of the statue is the ashes.

The distinctive culture of Brittany found expression in the many local costumes. All areas had their own costume, topped off by the head-dress, the coiffe, made of finest lace and shaped according to the region it represented. Like all Celtic people, the favoured musical instrument was the bagpipes, played at the religious processions, the 'pardons', held every year in various towns, where the people paraded to the church in local costume, to the accompaniment of the bagpipes, assaulting the ears of any non-Celts in the audience!

This, then, was the area in which I was to spend my year, an area which in so many ways was like home. I was to be living in St Brieuc, a small town on the north coast, which, in 1960, was small, provincial and no bigger than Banbury is today. It boasted only one main street and no really fashionable shops. It was the centre for the rural area about, children came in from the villages to

Medieval House
in Rue Fardel, St Brieuc

school, adults came to work and the shops catered for the rural pursuits of the inhabitants. It was picturesquely set with deep valleys on the outskirts and with its own sleepy little port, Le Légué, where we used to go swimming. The main square was dominated by the massive fortress cathedral of St Etienne, more powerful than beautiful, that spoke of the area's turbulent past. There were a few medieval houses, tucked away in a backstreet, but most of the town was solid bureaucratic France, where all the official buildings looked like military establishments, stiff, formal, and seemingly everlasting.

There was in the town no night-life. We walked home from the cinema late at night through darkened streets, past silent, shuttered houses, in an eerie silence. There were no fashionable restaurants: the preferred establishment was 'Pic Assiette , the no-nonsense, value for money cafe, into which everybody crammed at lunchtime, to be served steak and chips, sausages and chips and where the order and the bill were written on the paper tableclothes, and totted up

Cathedral of St Etienne, St Brieuc

afterwards, before the paper was cleared and renewed, ready for the next customer. Typical Breton fare, crêpes (pancakes) could be had in a bewildering variety of guises, in a little cafe opposite the cathedral, where you could watch the world go by as you ate to your heart's content. Now, St Brieuc is a traffic-choked and motorway cursed, bustling centre, but then it had the pace of life we so often crave for now, when life went on at a human pace, and nobody wanted to get anywhere particularly quickly.

Costumes
of Quimperlé

Quoiffe
of Bigouden

CHAPTER SIX

The School

When I got off the train at St Brieuc, at the beginning of October 1960, it was with a feeling of dread. I was worried about how I was going to manage to speak French all the time, whether I would be accepted and how I'd cope teaching French students. More immediately, as I stood on the almost empty, windswept platform, I wondered how on earth I was going to get to the school where I was going to spend the next year. So naive was I about travel arrangements, I who hadn't really been anywhere much in my life, that it hadn't entered my head to let them know when I would be arriving, so it was hardly surprising that there was no welcoming committee at the station to greet me. In a strange place, with no clear idea of how I was going to get on, or what awaited me, I felt particularly feeble and helpless. However, salvation came in the welcome form of the headmaster of the village school at Ploeuc, a small village just outside St Brieuc. I had travelled from St Malo with a young man from Walsall, who was destined for the village school at Ploeuc, and it was my luck that his Headmaster had turned up to fetch him from the station, for he it was who took pity on me and agreed to drop me off at my school on his way to Ploeuc. I was duly dropped off outside the big grille-gated entrance to the school, the headmaster went in to inform the Concierge that I had arrived and then he drove off with a cheery wave, leaving me feeling like an aristocrat, about to make his acquaintance with the guillotine.

The Ecole Normale des Filles, the girls' college, was a building of daunting size, a military-looking stone building, built on three sides of a square, the fourth side consisting of high iron railings with a small grille gate let into them to allow entrance to the building. The facade was punctuated by symmetrically set windows, with a large clock in the centre, topped off by a flagpole from which flew the tricolore. It was

Ecole Normale, St Brieuc

easy to see the influence of Napoleon in such buildings: it looked like a barracks. One could all too easily imagine the end of a lesson being announced by a roll on the drums, as it had been up till the beginning of this century. In the courtyard at the front was a small formal garden, with flower beds intersected by dusty gravel paths that seemed to lead nowhere but to each other.

The entrance was on the left, almost at the end of the left arm of the building, and it was guarded by that peculiarly French character, the concierge (caretaker). Concierges in France come in one of two basic patterns. The first is the genial, garrulous, jolly gossip, often to be met with sweeping the steps of the building or the pavement out front, and is usually only too willing to lean on her broom and pass on the gossip and news of the neighbourhood, as the chief informant of the bush telegraph of the area and a fount of knowledge on all things local. The second type is the morose, narrow-lipped detector of all abuses, real or imagined, a veritable Cerberus who guards her building with suspicious ferocity, crouching in her lair only to spring out like a vengeful harpy to savage any stranger who dares to violate the sanctity of her domain.

Unfortunately, Henriette was of this second type. I never

really knew her name: to her face we all referred to her respectfully as 'Madame', but behind her back she was always known as 'Henriette'. She was a short, dark, squat little figure, very Celtic looking, with lank grey hair, which she confined to a hairnet and which lay flat as a pancake on top of her head, crowning a permanent scowl. She bustled about officiously, performing her duties to the letter, terrified of being found wanting in the execution of her duty. She locked the grille gate with military precision every night at 9pm, and to be even a few seconds late would have her casting exaggeratedly fearful glances about her like a suspect in a poor thriller as she turned the key protestingly in the lock. This done, she would thrust the enormous key into the pocket of her pinafore and then scuttle back up the steps and into the building, shutting and locking the door after her, with much grating of bolts and clicking of locks, as she hermetically sealed the college for the night.

No-one could escape her vigilance. At the least sound of the front door opening she would come chugging out of her little office, like an asthmatic steam train, to see who was trespassing on her territory. Many a time I'd tiptoe down the hall, hoping to escape detection, only to hear her panting after me, crying,

"Mademoiselle Miss! Mademoiselle Miss!"

(she never learned my name, either!)

"You owe me ten francs!"

demanding payment for letters that my English friends had sent without the correct postage!

Inside, the school was an odd mixture of the grand and the utilitarian. The floors were stone, producing eerie echoes when we clicked over them in high heels in the dark after a night out.

Just inside the main entrance was a plain, stone-floored passage, with uncomfortable wooden benches all down one side. This was the 'parloir' , the hall where any unexpected visitor had to wait, while the girl he had come to visit was sent for. The girl would then speak to her visitor, in full earshot and view of any passerby (not to mention the ever-vigilant Henriette!). Visitors, as you can see, were not welcomed and therefore rare.

From the parloir, one passed through huge double doors to the 'galeries', a kind of glass conservatory cum passage, which went right round the inner part of the school, and from which radiated the classrooms. The galeries looked out onto a dispiriting yard which, later on was further reduced in size by the erection of a temporary classroom, leaving room only for a dusty basketball court, with neglected looking rusty hoops and ragged nets.

Downstairs, all of the doors were those high double doors you see in films set in the days of the French Revolution and the broad flights of stone steps that led to the upper floor were just like a set for 'The Count of Monte Cristo'. When you came to the upper floor, however, which housed the dormitories, you were in for a disappointment, for all you found was scuffed wooden doors, painted roughly in some drab colour, which opened to reveal large Spartan dormitories, whose only refinement were curtains of a cheap garish pattern, which could be pulled round each bed to allow a modicum of privacy, like in hospital wards at home. What puzzled me most about the dormitories was that the lavatory was outside, and yet the dormitories were locked at night. How anyone ever went to the lavatory during the night I never discovered.

I was to be accommodated in the school, in a small room right on the very tip of one of the arms of the building. It had two windows, one overlooking the street, the other looking down on the garden in front of the building. It had been an old isolation room and so was well away from the bustle of the dormitories. This part of the building was overseen by the school nurse, Mme Noiset, a kindly Breton woman who dispensed advice, sympathy and herbal tea in equal measures to the girls. They often called at bedtime for a calming tisane and a reassuring chat, especially just before exam time. She lived in the school all week, going home to her house in a little village outside St Brieuc only at weekends, to see her husband, who held a similar post in a boys' school, leaving only the weekends for them to pursue some kind of domestic life.

My room, painted a uniform, pale clinical blue, was sparsely furnished, with a naked light bulb hanging from an enormous flex from a high ceiling. There was a narrow bed, pushed up against the wall by the door, and with its traditional sausage-shaped pillow , without a pillow case but neatly wrapped in the end of the bottom sheet and tucked in to prevent it from coming unwrapped. There was a somewhat rickety wooden table that had seen better days and an arthritic-looking wooden chair, which, by a judicious process of petty theft had grown to three by the end of my stay. Under one of the windows sat a fat arm-chair, strangely patterned in brown and white. Being too vain to wear my glasses and being inconveniently short-sighted meant that until I actually sat in it I didn't realise the strange pattern came from its being a real cow-skin, the covering, I supposed, for many dinners past. It was distinctly and disconcertingly furry and reminded me in a gruesome way of Bobby, my Gran's cross-Spaniel dog, who was similarly patched in brown and white. A cupboard with shelves, of uncertain vintage, made up the sum total of my furniture. For some time I had nowhere to hang my clothes, but finally I was grudgingly provided with an ancient wardrobe which turned out to be something of a poisoned chalice, since it was wide but unnaturally shallow, which made it impossible to remove any garment from it without bringing the whole thing toppling over on me and pinning me embarrassingly to the floor.

The floor was bare boards, which were nursed to a high gloss by the rather quaint method of the cleaning-girl strapping to her feet two stiff brushes, and then skating over the floor, rubbing the boards to a high shine, a process she cheerfully informed me was called 'frotter le parquet'. In fact, this was a very dangerous practice, for to step on the bedside rug after one of her polishing sessions was tantamount to inviting death, and many a time I did a passable impression of Laurel and Hardy as I slipped and skidded across the floor, arms waving like windmill sails and eyes wild, trying to keep myself from crashing to the hard floor.

I was glad to see that my room boasted a wash basin, but was badly misled by the sight of two taps into believing that the place had hot water. In fact we had hot water in our rooms only once a week, hence the sight every Wednesday evening of every girl with her hair in curlers. Next door to my room was what I took to be my own personal lavatory. It was, in fact, the staff toilet, which was kept locked so that the girls could not use it, but the staff had a key. The room was merely a long, narrow corridor, at the end of which, beneath the small window, sat the toilet itself, in splendid isolation. It was so far from the door that should a member of staff come and try to unlock it, find it bolted from the inside, and go away without remembering to unlock it again, the occupant would be left in the same unenviable position as the now legendary three old ladies. After this had happened to me a couple of times, I took to always taking my key in with me, having grown tired of hanging from the window, calling for help in a French accent much distorted by embarrassment.

Downstairs by the kitchens were the showers, an uninviting row of cubicles, painted a depressing green and which worked but fitfully, either boiling you alive or freezing you solid, depending on how recently they had been in use. As a member of staff I was allowed to shower whenever I wished, but the girls went in strict rotation, only a few times a week. However, when I heard of the trials and tribulations of other students, also in France for their year, I thought I'd got off lightly. One of my friends was accommodated in a bedroom, converted from a ground-floor office by the addition of a bed and a cupboard. It was a modern building, with large windows, but no-one had thought it necessary to provide curtains, so she woke up every morning to find a sea of little faces peering at the strange foreign lady.

Tired of such public scrutiny, she demanded that curtains be provided and was directed to the proper authority, namely the

Town Hall! She finally got her curtains, or at least a roll of hideously patterned cheap curtain material, which she was obliged to attach to the windows by drawing pins, having no facilities for making the curtains up, which, as you may imagine, apart from being aesthetically most unpleasing, rendered her room, as Milton once said, "Dark, dark, dark, amid the blaze of noon."

An Ecole Normale, which took girls from the age of 16, was a training college, turning out, after a four year course, primary and nursery school teachers. They were first prepared for their Baccalaureat, the equivalent of GCSE and when they had passed that, they went on to learning how to teach, spending their last year in teaching practice in local schools. The course lasted four years, in principle, but in practice it could stretch out interminably, for, should a girl fail her Baccalaureat, she had to go on resitting it until she either passed or gave up trying and left. All the girls were boarders, sleeping in the dormitories, and following a punishing daily routine. Breakfast was at 7am, lessons began at 8 o'clock and went on till midday, with only a short break at 11 o'clock. Lunch was followed by more lessons until 4pm when tea was served - pieces of dry bread and jam or a piece of chocolate, whereupon they went back to their lessons until 5 or even 6 o'clock. After dinner at 7pm, they settled down at tables in the galeries to do their homework, then, after half an hour of recreation, they were sent to bed at 9pm.

The dormitories were supervised by surveillantes, a job that doesn't exist in English schools. They were a sort of paid prefect, girls in their late teens mostly, who were offered bed, board and a wage in exchange for a couple of days off a week to go up to Rennes to take a degree course at the university. It was a popular job amongst students, open only to girls who had themselves been educated in an Ecole Normale. Since grants for university students were almost unheard of, it was a perfect solution to the problem of how to pay their way through college. They did all the clerical jobs in the college, for the teachers did nothing but teach. If a teacher wanted a

class-list, someone to sit with a class while they did exams, a
form list for exam marks and percentages, the surveillantes
provided them and helped the Headmistress's secretary at
other times. They also looked after the girls in the dormitories
at night and kept order about the college.

The college was virtually a closed institution and the girls
were very closely supervised. They were not even allowed to
receive mail unless each letter was signed on the back by the
sender, who had to appear on a list of correspondents
approved by the girl's parents. They had lessons on Saturday
morning, but had Thursday afternoons free. This did not
mean that they could do as they liked, for, unless an
acceptable visitor came to take them out, they had to stay in
college, and even those who were taken out had to be back by
6pm. They were allowed out entirely unaccompanied only
once a year, just before Christmas, to buy their Christmas
presents in the town. Those who had no-one to take them out
on Thursday afternoon, were gathered together and taken
out, like a group of infants, on a supervised walk, with
surveillantes leading the procession and me bringing up the
rear, with strict instructions to prevent them from engaging in
unseemly conversation with unsuitable people en route
(usually young men). On some Sunday afternoons we took the
girls to the cinema, but if they were allowed to go to the
cinema on a weekday evening, they had to go to bed the next
night half an hour earlier, to catch up the sleep they had lost.

It was, indeed, a very closed society. It was rumoured that
the boys in their college on the other side of town, climbed out
of the windows at night and over the railings to go and make
whoopee in the town, but any such shocking behaviour as this
by the girls would have had their parents sent for to take
home their errant daughter. Actually, it was difficult for them
not to conform, for some of the staff also lived in. The
Principal, Mme Cholet, had an apartment in the school, where
she lived with her husband and children, as did the Domestic
Burser, Mme Argenton. The teachers came in from outside,
some of them teaching in more than one school in the town,

and some of them stayed in college for lunch.One of the teachers, Mme Le Gonidec, a tiresome woman with the sharp beak and the quick, jerky movements of a parrot, was a particular trial to me, for, in spite of all the evidence to the contrary, she persisted in the conviction that I spoke no French and, discussed me embarrassingly at table with all the other people, as if I were invisible. If I refused some food, she would ask,

"Doesn't she like that?"

or if the talk turned to holidays she would enquire of no-one in particular,

"Did she go away this holiday?"

smirking at me in a pitying way, as I grimaced mutely at her.

Under the rules governing assistant language teachers we were supposed to teach no more than 12 hours a week, to small groups of students. It was supposed to help children learn oral English from a native speaker. In practice, however, this rule was open to many interpretations. One of my friends, for example, regularly found herself in charge of 60 young children, but, to my delight, I found that I was looked upon by the Principal of my college as being more of a decoration than a working model of an English teacher, and for several weeks after my arrival she firmly refused to give me even a timetable, saying every time I met her about the college,

"I hope you're getting out and seeing something of Brittany." as if I were to be the eternal tourist.

When I did, finally, receive my timetable, it couldn't have been easier. I had only 11 hours of lessons a week, with groups of 5 or 6 students, for half an hour at a time. I was told by the English teacher merely to try to interest them in England and in things English, and to encourage them to speak the language. They were quite happy looking at pictures and posters which I had procured from the British Council, coloured pictures of London monuments, historic cities, the Royal Family and the like, but to get them to say a single word in English was another matter altogether. I struggled on for some time, trying to prise a single word of recognisable

English from their resolutely closed lips, while lessons
remained very silent affairs. Finally, in desperation, I tried
another tack. I spoke to them in French.

Transformation! These logs of dead wood I'd been
addressing all this time suddenly sparked into life. They
chatted, laughed, joked and lessons picked up no end. So this
is how we went on, my speaking French and they coming out
with the odd word of English. In all honesty, it did nothing at
all for their oral English, but my French improved no end.
Haunted by the feeling that I wasn't really doing my job, I
finally hit on a great idea. Spring was coming and the weather
was beginning to pick up, so I promised to take them out for
walks during lesson times (strictly against the rules, of
course), if they promised to speak only English en route. To
my amazement, the ploy worked; they'd do anything to get out
a bit and, although at first the walks were strangely silent
affairs, after a while they unbent enough to try out their
English and make a real effort. The only trouble was that by
this time I had begun to forget English myself. I thought in
French, dreamed in French, talked to myself in French and
often had to ask the girls to provide me with an English word
that had inconveniently escaped my memory!

So the time passed, and all would have been perfect, had it
not been for awful 8am lessons I had to endure. Giving lessons
in the dead of winter, when it was still pitch dark outside and
cheerless indoors depressed me. After all, a radiator doesn't
give out any comforting glow on a bleak winter's morning.
After I had appeared for lessons at 8 am several times, only to
be told that the pupils couldn't come because they had
practical science lessons or exams, I rebelled. From now on, I
decided, I would give the early morning lessons from the
comfort of my bed. After all, the French King Louis XIV had
instituted the tradition of the 'grande levée', when his rising
from his bed was witnessed by privileged courtiers. Anyway, I
had just the incentive to attract students to the idea - I had an
electric kettle and the power point was right next to my bed.
Coffee and biscuits would be just the thing to help along

English conversation at an unearthly time of the morning. From then onwards I was to be seen, sitting up in bed, the bed strewn with maps, pictures and posters, and surrounded by animated students, drinking steaming cups of reviving coffee and imbibing great dollops of English culture. Then, lesson over, I could retreat beneath the blankets and doze peacefully until a more civilised time of the morning, whereupon I would rise and take a stroll round the town before lunch.

Lady Luck was determined, so it seemed, to smile upon me, for, to all this life of proverbial Riley was added yet another benefit. During the year the English teacher left to go on maternity leave and I was asked to take over the English lessons for the first year pupils, for which I would be paid extra. I was already paid the same as the surveillantes and was charged for my bed, board, laundry and room-cleaning the paltry sum of £9 a month, so, for the first time in my life, I was rich. And all I had to do was to take the class of the Seconde for a few lessons a week.

It is a standing joke in Britain that the French education system is so rigid that at any given time of day you can say with certainty what every child in France is doing in every class. It may not be true now, but it was in 1960. All the textbooks and contents of lessons were prescribed by the government, even, in some cases, how many minutes per lesson were to be devoted to a particular exercise. The English text book for my girls was odd in the extreme. Its reading passages dealt with Red Indians travelling down untamed rivers by canoe, or South African farmers riding on horseback through the veldt country, but about England and the English there was nothing. They could all say, "The Indian brave got into his canoe", but they couldn't ask their way into the next street! Their English was comically old-fashioned: 'fainted' was inevitably 'swooned', 'people' were always 'persons' - they were more attuned to the world of Victorian misses than to that of the modern girl!

Being only temporary I had no fear of being denounced by the dreaded Inspectors for not following the correct curriculum, so I used to finish every lesson with pronunciation practice, getting the girls who, being French, couldn't pronounce 'h', to chant all together, "Oh, Horace, isn't it horrid, when you're hot and in a hurry, to have to hold your hat on with your hanky in your hand", or "round and round the rugged rock the ragged rascal ran" as an encouragement to produce an English 'r', rather than a French one, which always reduced lessons to uproarious laughter.

Actually, my lessons were all too prone to be reduced to farce, and I was frequently left looking for my dignity. In the room where I taught, the teacher's desk was raised up on a little wooden dais in front of the blackboard. I, who was always clad in fashionable tight skirt and very high heeled shoes, found it almost impossible to climb on the dais and tottered about on it in my high heels, trying to interest the girls more in what I said than in what a spectacle I presented. One day, I was writing on the blackboard, explaining, I hoped with great authority, some fascinating point of grammar, as I wrote, walking from one end of the board to the other. Unfortunately, unknown to me, the platform upon which I was consisted of two pieces of wood, which had somehow worked slightly apart, leaving a gap between them. As I stepped along, suddenly, one of my high heels disappeared down the crack, pitching me unceremoniously onto the floor, behind the teacher's desk, and out of view of the pupils. As I sat there, nursing my bruised pride, I was startled to hear a deathly silence take possession of the room. On hands and knees I peered nervously round the desk to see what was going on, to find them all desperately trying not to laugh and going purple in the face with the effort. The sight of my equally beetroot red face, peek-a-booing at knee height round the side of the desk was finally too much for them, and we all collapsed in gales of laughter.

Somehow, lessons were never the same again after that!

CHAPTER SEVEN

Social Life

Being one of very few foreigners in a town gives you an unwarranted importance which can be very useful socially. In St Brieuc there were only four British people; the four assistants at the schools, and consequently we were well known in the town, and were often invited to official functions as being foreign guests, who must be shown hospitality. Surprisingly enough, this didn't mean that we met very much socially apart from this, partly because the girl from the girls' school was engaged to a Frenchman and spent every spare moment with him, and partly because the man from the boys' college had a strange view of what constituted a social life. Humphrey Lloyd Humphreys was a Liverpool-Welshman, tall, thin, pale and sandy haired, with a large ginger moustache that projected so far from his skinny frame as to have earned him the nickname "The Crucifix" from his students. His passion was his Celtic heritage and he had learned Breton in six months, even speaking French with a Breton accent.

He spent all his spare time chugging about the remote countryside on his moped, engaging the peasants out in the fields in conversation in Breton. As a social companion for anyone else, however, he was useless. He fell asleep at the cinema and to accept an invitation to take coffee with him at his place meant an evening of listening to records of a 73 year old Breton woman singing, in cracked and tremulous tones, ancient Breton folk songs, while Humphrey sat enraptured, a beatific look on his face.

My chief companions in social engagements were the surveillantes at my school, of whom there were four. Denise was particularly useful, as we'd joined a club that showed films of geographical or travel interest, which were shown at a local cinema. Unfortunately, every club you joined entailed a membership card, endorsed with your photograph and which was checked closely at every meeting, a laborious and time-consuming pastime. Luckily for us,however, one of the cinema employees had conceived a great, if entirely unrequited, passion for Denise and used to let us in the back door, in the hope of catching a few words with her. Pierrette, the oldest of the surveillantes, was married and expecting her first baby, so her social life was much curtailed. Her husband was doing his national service (all young men had to do 27 months of national service) in the army, stationed at Chartres, so Pierrette whiled away the time before Yvon's demobilisation and the birth of her child, sitting quietly in her room, knitting prodigious amounts of the obligatory tiny garments for the expected baby. As time went on, she grew so large that she grumbled good-naturedly that if we put a ribbon round her middle she could do duty as an Easter egg!

Claudie, vivacious, dark and attractive, had little time for social life with the rest of us, for she was at that time deeply embroiled in a breathlessly hot affair with the son of a local baker. I suppose it wasn't surprising, really, for, the tight regime of school, with hardly any outings and no meetings with the opposite sex meant that once they were pushed out into the world, into the free and easy life of the university, they were inclined to go quite mad. So, many parents sat in their suburban or rural respectability, fondly believing that their children were being supervised as closely as they had been at school, while all the time their newly liberated offspring were living it up on the days they spent in Rennes, creating for themselves love lives of a complexity that would have done credit to the intrigues of a medieval court. Claudie's life was certainly a veritable swamp of alternating passion and guilt; regular crises, emotional turmoil, spectacular quarrels with her lover, pregnancy scares and a desperate quest to be just what he wanted of her, so he would marry her and make the deception and the emotional roller-coaster unnecessary. Under his influence, she gave up attending social functions, dressed in the sombre colours he decreed, settled into a life resembling that of a novice nun,

all in the cause of stilling his jealousy long enough to make
him marry her, while continuing to live with him for three
nights of unbridled passion every week in Rennes, which
made for spectacular highs and catastrophic lows that
reduced us all to something resembling a wrung-out
dishcloth.

My chief companion was Paulette, who regularly invited
me to spend weekends with her family in their home at
Perros-Guirec, the seaside resort on the pink granite coast.
They lived in a small bungalow, built of pink granite, with
window sills of contrasting grey granite. It hardly looked
real: it was like the ginger-bread house of the fairy story.
Here, I was accepted as one of the family, enjoying her
father's schoolboy humour, his puns, his awful jokes and his
hilarious and totally unsuccessful attempts to teach me to
tango in the narrow confines of the tiny living room, where
two suitably dramatic strides brought us slap up against the
opposite wall, whereupon we turned round and took two
more dramatic strides, amid much raucous laughter from
the rest of the family.

The Boys' College, on the other side of town, was built to
exactly the same pattern as that of the Girls', so I could call
there and be entirely at home, finding my way about the
building with uncanny accuracy. I was frequently invited
over for coffee by Jean, one of the surveillants, but since that
side of town appeared to have been untouched by
civilisation, I could only be sure of receiving any
refreshment after my long walk over there, if I took with me
my electric kettle, a jar of coffee and milk and sugar. Once,
in an effort to impress, they offered me a tin of pineapple
chunks, which we ended up eating out of teacups, with our
fingers, since they didn't run to refinements such as spoons!

As you can see, then, entertainment and social life was
very much a do-it-yourself affair, though it's surprising just
how many clubs and societies you can find to join in a small
town. We joined libraries, film clubs, lecture clubs, from
which, sometimes, all we seemed to gain was the patience of

a saint. One afternoon, having nothing to do, we attended what had been billed as an illustrated lecture on Tolstoy. As it turned out, the illustrations consisted of a few faded sepia photographs of the most dreary subjects, accompanied by a commentary of the most banal kind. A blurred picture of an old man with a long white beard (Tolstoy, no less), was accompanied by the inspired comment, "Tolstoy writing". Next we saw a shambling figure in a field, pushing an ancient wooden plough. Commentary: "Tolstoy ploughing". For what seemed an eternity we sat through this, yawning exaggeratedly and casting pointed glances at our watches, until, finally taking the hint, the speaker stuttered to a close. He asked us, hopefully, if we had any questions and, to our amazement and rage, some rash youth put up his hand, but before he could say anything, he was seized from behind by an enraged neighbour, who hissed in his ear, "Shut up, idiot!" which enabled us to make our escape.

Much of our entertainment we got from events at the schools, concerts, plays and the end of year Gala, where the boys joined with the girls to offer singing, acting and music. For our girls, the highlight of the year was the annual dance, which took place in the school hall, and to which, naturally, the boys were invited. The dancing began in the afternoon and, with a break for tea and to get back one's stamina, resumed in the evening. Dancing in France, I discovered, had very little to do with Victor Sylvester and strict tempo, for the chief step seemed to consist of a rather half-hearted shuffle from one foot to the other, moving round in ever decreasing circles until you felt dizzy and had to stop for refreshment. The only other favoured dance seemed to be the passa doble, a wild Spanish affair in which you take long, dramatic strides, change direction with remarkable and unpredictable sharpness and stamp with as much vigour as possible on everybody's feet.

Dancing was a particular trial to me since I am rather tall and Breton men, typically, are small, so I often found myself to be head and shoulders above my partners, which left me, as the French say, looking round the room like a lighthouse, with my partner's head jammed uncomfortably under my chin. One day, to the girls' obvious amusement, one of my partners solved the problem by seizing me in a vice-like grip around my neck as we danced, which bent me double, in a passable impression of the Hunchback of Notre Dame, as he dragged me about the dance floor like a rag doll.

On balance, the cinema was a safer pastime, although the girls' passion for Sacha Distel films did drive us to distraction. Sunday afternoons were the best times to go to the cinema, for the world and his wife went to the cinema then, and followed it by the pleasant social ritual of a stroll down the main street, where everyone met everyone they knew, hands were shaken and polite enquiries were made about health and family before everyone adjourned to the big patisserie and tearoom at the end of the street, which opened specially to serve tea and cakes. And what cakes! There were rhum babas, huge sticky islands, floating in an alcoholic sea; chocolate eclairs, long as barges, filled to the brim with a glorious chocolate cream that oozed out over your fingers if injudiciously poked with a pastry fork; rectangular mille feuilles, filled with a glorious custard and covered with a generous dusting of icing sugar, which came off onto everything it touched - fingers, table, cheeks; and Breton galettes, flat as dinner plates, like slates off the roof of a gingerbread house. Then, gluttonous over-indulgence over for another week, we would climb up the hill back to the school, consoling ourselves that it really was only a venial sin, and we'd have school meals the next day to make up for it.

Actually, school meals weren't all that bad, although the girls grumbled about them all the time. I didn't like the dreaded salade (dressed lettuce) with every meal and have avoided it ever since, but I soon got used to being the cabaret for the girls at every mealtime as I tried to cope with unfamiliar foods. They cackled with laughter over my attempts to eat artichokes, which sat on the plate like huge, steaming hot green conkers, still in their prickly shells, daring you to touch them, let alone try to eat them. It still seems to me to be a lot of work for nothing, laboriously removing each leaf, dipping it in a sauce and biting off the tiny piece of flesh at the end, before several minutes of work leave you with the fleshy heart to eat. Tinned pears were also something of a hazard since, in France, they are not soft and squashy as in England, but hard as bricks. My clumsy efforts to cut one with my spoon, sent it shooting off the plate, across the table and over the other side of the dining hall, where it came to rest under a table full of giggling girls.

I didn't get to grips with the famous frogs' legs, but I did eat snails. Paulette's mother was determined that I should try them and prepared them one weekend when I was visiting. Much amusement was gained at my expense, with comments such as, "We got them from our own garden, you know", and "we have to keep them for three weeks before we eat them". I was left with only the time-honoured advice (though usually given in another context!) to close my eyes and think of England, to keep me from public disgrace. They were brought in with some ceremony, hot and steaming on a large dish, and were distributed equally between us. Then an expectant silence fell upon the table, as everyone waited for me to begin.I was solemnly handed a long-handled fork with two prongs with which to impale the monster in its shell, which I did, swallowing it straight down. To my relief, it all turned out to be something of an anti-climax: it didn't taste of anything, really, except the garlic it was cooked in. It was all rather like chewing bits of tasteless indiarubber. Still, I had defended the honour of England and lived to tell the tale.

But, of course, France is not only noted for food; it is a fashion centre, so I next turned my attention to clothes. I had never owned any decent clothes: at home I'd often had to borrow a pair of shoes from my mother to be able to go out for an evening, so I didn't intend to waste the opportunity to spend my money on something decent to wear, while I could.

In 1960 clothes in France were fiendishly expensive, compared with at home. I regularly paid £12 for shoes that would have cost no more than £3 in England, and the ready-to-wear market was not nearly as well developed in France as in England. To my delight I discovered that it made good economic sense to have my clothes made to measure by that legendary figure, who had long since disappeared from the English scene - the little dressmaker round the corner. Thanks to Claudie I made the acquaintance of the miraculous Mme Vallée, who lived literally just round the corner and was a veritable wizard with a needle and thread. I had only to call on her and describe exactly what I wanted, provide her with the amount of material she said I would need, and the next time I went to see her, there would be my exact garment, made up and ready for me to try on. She said she loved making clothes for us young people, because most of her clients were old and fat, with a predilection for purple velvet, and she really did us proud. She created all her own patterns and all her clothes were lined and hand finished by her apprentice, a mouse of a child, no more than 16, who sat in a corner all day, quietly sewing, lining skirts, inserting zips and sewing on hooks and eyes. (Mme Vallée wouldn't have buttons: she said they spoilt the line of skirts). Thanks to her, during the year, I built up a whole wardrobe of clothes that would have done credit to a fashion house. It was all a bit like Cinderella, before the clock struck midnight!

Transformed as I was: fashionable clothes, modern hairstyle, courtesy of Mme Ancelin, the hairdresser recommended by Claudie to transform me, it was difficult to remember that I'd been sent to France to study and to further my education. When I'd left England it was with exhortations from Professor Sykes to write literary essays to keep myself in practice, to devour the quality newspapers to help improve my own French style and to enrol at the nearest university for some academic course. From time to time I received letters from him, all kindness and concern, hoping I was not neglecting my studies, to which I replied with dutiful phrases and vague descriptions of my industry, while, in truth, only using the university as a place to meet my friends and keep up my English in their English Club. Leicester seemed so very far away!

CHAPTER EIGHT

Travel

The winter of 1960-61 was unusually mild, and, true to the new and hedonistic search for enjoyment rather than duty, which had come over me in France, I wasted no opportunity for travel. In those innocent days this all too often meant hitch-hiking. We frequently hitch-hiked to Rennes to buy the dress material that Mme Vallée transformed into her haute couture creations and many of our best adventures came from taking to the road and trying our luck with hitching. During one holiday, Paulette and I decided we had to visit the Ile de Bréhat, a tiny island off the pink granite coast, a place of great beauty called locally 'the island of flowers'. To get to the place where we could catch a boat to the island we proposed to hitch a lift. This at first seemed to have been a bad idea, for, for some time we merely trudged down deserted roads towards the Pointe de l'Arcouest, where we could catch the ferry, in the heat of the day, with no vehicle in sight. Suddenly, a scruffy looking old Citroen stopped to offer us a lift, a car packed to the roof with a family of gypsies, dark, hairy and wild-looking. The car smelt of the farmyard, but grateful for any assistance, we crushed into the back, alongside numerous family members, unable to put our feet down on the floor of the car, which was occupied by numerous live chickens, legs tied together to prevent them from flying round the car and causing mayhem. They had obviously been recently purloined from some farm on route, and were being kept on the floor out of view, but we were in no position to complain, so we merely sat in the bedlam of squawking chickens, chattering children and the groans of the old car, protesting at carrying so much weight, until we thankfully reached the ferry point and were able to bid our benefactors goodbye and get out of the car, by this time reeking of the farmyard ourselves.

The tiny ferryboat steamed into the little sheltered

harbour of the island, defended by cliffs of bright pink granite, worn into grotesque shapes by the wind, and we wasted no time, starting with paddling in the shallow water of the harbour, watching tiny shrimps darting about in the clear water. We walked about the island, ablaze with flowers of every colour, looking at the old picturesque thatched cottages and their bright cottage gardens, before going into a restaurant to feast on the sea-food for which the island is famous: enormous, crackling langoustines, which had to be prised from their armour plating before we ate them, leaving huge piles of empty shells, like miniature suits of armour, littering the table; vast red lobsters whose past we didn't like to dwell upon, for hadn't we seen them only that morning, happy and alive, crawling about the large tank outside the fishmonger's shop in the town, blithely unaware of the cruel fate that awaited them come dinner time?

We were more than slightly apprehensive when we came to go home, given our difficulties in getting there, but we were grateful to be offered a lift in a Post Office van. It was one of those grey, corrugated tin-can looking vans, that seem to have been made by children in a craft lesson, from instructions given on 'Blue Peter', but it was certainly a step up from Noah's Ark, which had taken us to the island. Apart from bouncing up and hitting our heads on the roof of the van every time we went over a bump in the road, we arrived back in good order,with all kinds of happy memories stored away for future discussion.

For some reason we were fascinated by islands, perhaps because Brittany has so many of them, and one holiday, when I was staying in Redon, with an English friend, also doing her year in France, we decided we'd like to see Belle Ile, made famous by the books of Dumas. We took the train as far as Auray, intending to hitch-hike from there to Quiberon, the port on the tip of the isthmus sticking out into the Atlantic Ocean, where we could catch a boat for the island. After a journey of more than an hour we docked at Le Palais, the chief town of the island, where we decided that if we were to see all the island in a short space of time, some mechanical conveyance would be required. Although neither of us had ridden a bicycle since childhood, we hired a couple of antique machines cheaply and began pedalling up the steep hill that led out of the town. The machines were more antique than we had realised, for as soon as I pushed vigorously on one pedal, it promptly fell off, leaving me to struggle on like a mechanised Long John Silver. By sheer determination we rode our rusty steeds all round the island, looked down from steep cliffs into small rocky bays where clearly visible floated huge jelly-fish, which looked as big as dustbin lids. We walked through tangled grassland, alive with green lizards and lost ourselves in the sheer wildness and remoteness of the place. Finally, we rode back to Le Palais, our bicycles disintigrating further with every mile. Mine had no brakes and had to be stopped in an emergency by the time-honoured method of putting the foot into the front wheel, and the saddle of my friend's machine had by now assumed an angle which made it, if not dangerous, at least uncomfortable to sit down, but at least we had accomplished what we'd set out to do, to explore the island.

The return journey from Quiberon, however, proved to be something of a nightmare, for the first people to offer us a lift were as weird a couple as you could meet. One of them looked fairly normal, a callow youth of undistinguished features but disconcerting topics of conversation. The first thing he asked us as we set off was whether French boys ever attempted to take liberties with us when they found out that we were English. My friend, thinking that this was a prelude to his doing just that, seized her duffle bag firmly and prepared to strike him a mortal blow if he approached her, but he appeared to be quite satisfied with the thought alone, and sat there chuckling inanely and eyeing us with humour. His companion, a hunch-backed dwarf, who brought to mind all the terrors of fairy stories, chortled gleefully with the youth about our possible discomfiture and when they suddenly veered off the main road into a small narrow track, I, too, began to harbour fears about white slavery. As it turned out, they were only making a detour, to show us the standing stones at Carnac, the Celtic monuments akin to Stonehenge in Britain. But it was beginning to get dark by this time and the brooding presence of the stones, allied with our odd companions, began to alarm us somewhat and we took our leave of them, preferring to put up for the night in a small hotel in Rochefort en Terre, rather than risk meeting up with similar weirdos in the dark.

The third of our islands was the famous Mont St Michel, the much visited island, claimed by both Normandy and Brittany. This time we went by bus, eagerly looking through the front window as we neared the coast for our first glimpse of the Mont, rising from the sea like a beautiful vision, the narrow spire of the abbey crowning the forbidding looking wall, rising sheer from the rock from which it was carved, the outline standing stark against the backdrop of the blue sky and the sea that swirled restlessly about the base of the Mont. We drove across the causeway, which linked the Mont to the mainland, only passable at low tide, and entered the only gate to the walled village, guarded by massive medieval towers. We made our way tortuously up the side of the Mont, thronged as usual with tourists, up the single, steep, narrow, winding, cobbled street that led to the abbey at the top: up the narrow street, overhung by the upper storeys of the medieval buildings on each side; shops overflowing into the congested street, with bright, highly-coloured Breton pottery, clothes embroidered with the curls and swirls of traditional Celtic patterns, every souvenir, useful and useless, emblazoned with the legend: "A present from Mont St Michel". Upwards we toiled, past the large ladies, red-faced, leaning over their hot griddles, dispensing waffles and crêpes to order to the passers-by, finally arriving at the top, where we sought sanctuary from the heat in the majestic cool of the ancient abbey, cut from the solid rock which formed the Mont. We strolled round the beautiful cloisters,

admiring the delicate pillars and stone tracery, looking into
the sunbathed courtyard. We rested a while in the dignified
peace of the building, to get our breath back before making
the perilous descent, fighting against the tide of people
making their breathless way to the top, running the
gauntlet again of the eager shopkeepers, determined to sell
us every possible souvenir or a myriad of good things to eat.
Finally, we drove away, looking over our shoulders to catch
a last glimpse of the fairy-tale scene as it receded into the
distance like a mirage, rising like a vision from the sea,
totally unreal.

Lazy days spent on the beach at Val André, the smart
resort of the in-crowd of St Brieuc, and visits to the many
beauty spots had confirmed me in the pleasures of a life of
agreeable idleness and it seemed that the sun would shine
for ever. But, of course, it couldn't last and I had to return to
Leicester, to the serious business of getting my degree. I had
become so used to coffee black as pitch, served in cups as big
as swimming pools, to French bread so crusty that it seemed
to play havoc with the teeth and gums and to that
indefinable 'French smell' that assails your nostrils every
time you enter a public building - a mixture of French
cigarettes and standard issue polish - but now I had to go
back to being an ordinary, unremarkable student. In spite of
all my fears when I'd set out for France a year before, I'd just
spent the happiest year of my life, and I wasn't at all sure I'd
find it easy to settle back into student life.

CHAPTER NINE

The Last Lap

When we returned to university in October 1961 for our last year, we were treated to an indulgent smile from Professor Sykes, who commented wryly on our new-found sophistication. And we had changed - at least, I knew I had. Not only did I now speak fluent French, I'd experienced French life and culture at first hand, with all the benefits that exposure to the wider world inevitably brings, but also, for the first time in my life, I had a wardrobe of fashionable clothes, a hairstyle that no longer resembled a bird's nest, and a confidence to match. I hardly recognised myself as the mouse-like, ill-clad, awkward creature who'd arrived three years before, clutching a borrowed suitcase and weighed down with worries.

Still, there was no time for swanning about and showing off my newly acquired feathers: I had to start finding somewhere to live. After two years in a Hall of Residence, I was, for my last year, to be cast out to fend for myself. While I was away in France, all my contemporaries had finished their degrees and left, but I managed to find two friends, one from my own department and one who had stayed on to work in the university library, with whom to share a flat. All we had to do was find one. One friend was already working and living temporarily in a seedy bedsitter, while she waited for us to find something better together.

I stayed with her one night, with the aim of looking at properties together the following day and was thoroughly depressed to notice the straitened circumstances that led so many poor souls to live in her lodging house, their only home. The large, once-handsome Victorian house was divided into sordid little bed-sitters, all poorly furnished and offering no running water. All they had was a sink outside on the landing. For these, what the landlord laughably called 'services' they were charged exorbitant rents. It was a life of the utmost poverty. Particularly distressing was the plight of a couple I met on the stairs, a married couple nearing late middle age, who were eking out an existence in the squalor of this demoralising house. Their poky, ill-furnished room was all they had to call home, and it saddened me beyond measure to think how many people, long past the age when they might have been expected to have made their way in the world, were still living this sordid, hand-to-mouth existence. This was poverty such as even I had never known and I felt grateful that at least I had lived in a Council house, with a bathroom and several rooms to it. It depressed me to think that for so many people the rosy future was all behind them and nothing lay ahead.

Just round the corner from this unedifying lodging-house was a street of more large Victorian houses, whose gentility had been reduced by fading prosperity to conversion into flats and bed-sitters, the fate of so many beautiful throw-backs to a more affluent past. There, in 1 St. Peter's Road for the sum of £7 a week, we found a ground floor flat. By this time the three of us had grown to four, since one of the girls had married, so the flatmates became three girls and one man. The flat itself consisted of a large front room, with a wide bay window, which did duty as sitting-room and bedroom for two of the girls, a back bedroom for the married couple, a

1 St Peter's Road

tiny dining room and a small kitchen. The bathroom and toilet, on the first floor, had to be shared between all the residents of the house. The bathwater was supposed to be heated by an ancient Ascot heater, more likely to burst into flames than to heat water, so we usually preferred to bath in the Students' Union building. It seemed adequate otherwise, apart from the curtains in the living room, garish yellow and red striped cotton, a knock-down bargain at the market if ever I saw one.

It wasn't until we moved in that we discovered that we had made an elementary error in our eagerness to find a roof over our heads before term started - we had moved into a house of ill fame. It wasn't exactly a brothel - the girls were not organised by a pimp or a Madam; they were freelance, but, nevertheless, the rest of the house, divided into bed-sitters, was home to several girls whose clients incessantly rang the front door bell, which we, as the ground floor tenants, were more often than not forced to answer. Whatever we'd expected when we'd taken the flat it wasn't to be an answering service in a den of vice. Nevertheless, we ended up greeting clients and showing them upstairs. Most of the clients were coloured American servicemen from the big American base near Leicester. We soon became inured to opening the door to a bewildering variety of men, who greeted us with,

"Gee, thanks! I forgot my key!"

which persuaded us that half the population of Leicestershire had a key to our house!

We soon got to know the girls quite well. On the top floor lived Norma, whose story was a psychiatrist's dream. It appeared that she had once been happily and respectably married to a member of a famous male singing group of the 1950s, and enjoyed an exciting and affluent life-style. Unfortunately, during the course of his work, her husband had met and fallen in love with a member of an equally famous girls' group of the time and had left Norma for this woman. Her husband's totally unexpected defection had, so we were told, totally unbalanced Norma, who sank into prostitution - she'd become the archetypal 'good-time girl', like Holly Golightly. She was a truly beautiful girl, impeccably groomed and always dressed in the height of fashion: she looked more than a class above her trade. As we watched her disappearing down the street, high heels clicking jauntily on the pavement, we would opine sagely and rather sadly that it didn't seem fair, somehow, for such a lovely woman to have come to this, and all because of a man.

If Norma was as close to the stereotypical prostitute as is chalk to cheese, then Gloria, who lived on the first floor, was the stereotype to a T. She was a young girl of monumental brainlessness and bright orange hair, who purported for a time to work as a check-out girl in the little local supermarket, but soon found more lucrative outlets for her talents and abandoned the grocery store. Actually, Gloria wasn't so brainless as to be ever left in financial want: like many an alley-cat she always landed on her feet. She was, as we were soon to find to our cost, a member of a most successful shop-lifting gang, who specialised in stealing whole racks of expensive clothes from department stores, often unloading them, still on their racks, from an old van outside our window, under our open-mouthed incredulous gaze. Unfortunately, Gloria's cronies didn't confine their kleptomania to local stores, for one day, when the house was empty, they came in and went through all the belongings of the tenants. We, being just poor students, had virtually nothing to steal, of course, but they took our washing off the line and even one of our suitcases to carry away their ill-gotten gains. The girls also lost personal items, which aroused in them, as it had in us, most vengeful feelings. They, however, had more chance of doing something about it than we had. The local underworld was alerted and several days later we received a mysterious message concerning a left luggage locker at London Road railway station. Investigation of the said locker revealed much of our stolen property, except, I was particularly aggrieved to discover, my new pyjamas, which had been purloined from the washing line.

After this little episode, Gloria, feeling herself to be *persona non grata* in the house, prudently decamped. Encouraged by her American clients, she took off with a friend to Germany, to settle near another American Air Force base and offer her services to a whole new group of eager clients. For several months we received postcards from her, bearing the mocking legend,
"Wish you were here!"
and finally, after her foray abroad, she returned, infinitely richer, to settle locally again.

The third girl, whom we came to know well, was Janet, the most intelligent and complex of the girls. She found work for a while as an auxiliary in a hospital, work which she enjoyed, but she couldn't break away from her former life and associates - she, too, like Norma, was undone by a man. Neither Gloria nor Norma had one particular man, but Janet was most messily entangled with an American serviceman known as Evans. He had a wife and family back home in America, but that didn't stop him from ruining Janet's life as well. He was a brutal man, who treated her shamefully. If he chose not to give her any money (which happened frequently), then she existed on what food we sent up for her - for several weeks, when funds were low for us all, we all lived on huge helpings of spaghetti. Once Evans relented, and gave her money, we all got a change of diet!

Weekends, when they had all been drinking, was the time for partying and violence. Music would be turned on full blast, dancing would begin in the room above ours, which sounded like people treading grapes above our heads, while we cowered in our beds, heads under the blankets, trying to get some sleep. After a while, the shrieks of raucous laughter would take on a more sinister tone, voices raised in anger, along with sundry bangs and crashes, whereupon record players, plus any movable furniture and unwanted personnel would come tumbling down the stairs, where we would find it, in various states of disrepair, lying in the hall the following morning.

That fun over, Evans always took to beating Janet. We, scandalised by the treatment she seemed to accept so meekly, instructed her, the moment Evans began to show signs of aggression, to abandon him and flee downstairs to take refuge with us behind our locked door. Whether the ensuing scenes were comic or tragic I haven't really made up my mind, but many a weekend saw the ludicrous sight of Evans banging furiously on our door, like some enraged buffalo, describing in graphic detail and colourful language what he would do to both Janet and us, should he finally get his eager hands upon us, while we cowered cravenly behind the mercifully solid door, shouting at him, with a good deal more bravado than we felt, to go away and leave Janet alone. Such was the original morality that pertained in our house that once, Janet, finally tired of Evans's persistent abuse of her, went down the road at dead of night and fetched her husband out of bed with another woman to come and order Evans to treat her more kindly!

The sad fact, however, was that Janet, for reasons known only to herself, was totally locked into this cycle of abuse, and when Evans learnt that he was to be transferred to a base in Germany, she even made plans to follow him there. In vain did we try to dissuade her from this hare-brained scheme, pointing out that when his tour of duty was over he would just return to his family in America, abandoning her in a foreign country whose language she didn't speak. Before this event took place, however, we left Leicester, so we never found out what happened to that sad girl.

But it wasn't all gloom. Gloria and Evans, for some reason, were bitter enemies, and their crossing of swords often gave us lighter moments. Gloria never seemed to be organised enough to pay her bills when due and at one time had failed to pay her television rental for several weeks, always managing to be out, or well hidden when the man called for his money. Evans, delighted by her discomfiture, left a most unsympathetic note on her door one day, to whit, "Ha ha! Pay up or else!" which sent Gloria into such paroxysms of rage that she took herself off in a huff, doing her equivalent of a moonlight flit, to avoid both Evans and the television man alike. Only, with all the commonsense we had come to expect from Gloria, she went no further than into the next street, where one didn't need to be Sherlock Holmes to track her down!

With Gloria gone, life was quieter in 1 St Peter's Road, for into her room moved, not another girl, but a couple. They rode a motorcycle, wearing matching leathers and crash-helmets, and they were as alike a two peas. They were both small, with short blond curls, and reminded me irresistibly of the little weather man and lady who came out from their little house to tell whether it was going to be wet or fine. Looking at them always brought to mind the thought that there must be a God, since He'd so obviously made these two for each other: they were like a matching cruet set. They led a life as quiet and unobtrusive as Gloria's had been explosive, and the man was eminently useful to us in braving the spooky cellar to mend the fuses, which blew with tiresome regularity.

Then, one night, this quiet and unremarkable tenor of life suddenly came to an abrupt end. The first sign of trouble was the sound of a noisy altercation going on in the hall. As we went out, curious to see what was going on, we saw the woman, fleeing in panic up the stairs, gasping breathlessly, "It's my husband!"

On the doorstep stood a man we took to be her vengeful spouse, who had finally caught up with his errant wife and her lover. So, it was off to pastures new for them, and our last sight of them was their motor cycle disappearing at full speed down the road, their blond curls peeping coyly from beneath their matching helmets, leaving us to cope with our own fuses.

It may be supposed that, with all the excitement and

distractions at home, we didn't have time to be students as well, but, of course, we had to. The American servicemen continued to be an ever-present distraction: they introduced us to the music of Ray Charles and planned wild parties in our flat (which, mercifully, never materialised), and, although we didn't go out much, we did see life. At weekends we ran the gauntlet of a constant stream of strangers and to tap nervously on the door of one of the girl's rooms of an evening, in search of change for the electricity meter would more often than not get us dragged into a wild, excited group of people, in various states of undress, offering us drinks and other attentions. Over at college, on the other hand, life pursued its usual sedate way.

The first hurdle to get over after our return was to attend the dreaded interview with Professor Sykes, when he reviewed our year abroad and delivered his verdict on our performance while out of his care and scrutiny for a year. My interview, to my astonishment, went off remarkably well, considering how little academic study I had to offer for his perusal. This was mainly thanks to the fact that while in France I had run an English choir, and my descriptions of the girls on the bus to the sports field every week, accompanied by raucous renditions of their favourite English song, "Old McDonald had a Farm", complete with noisy animal noises, tickled him enough to make him forget my very real deficiencies and concentrate on my conspicuous successes!

We soon got back into the old routine of weekly proses, translations, essays, and the necessity for defending your views, however shaky and untenable, in tutorials with irritatingly intrusive lecturers, skilled in the art of the third degree. But there was a difference, somehow. A year away had changed me. I'd grown up, I suppose, and being a student again after a wonderful year of freedom wasn't so appealing. One reason for the change of heart was, no doubt, that changing from Hall to a flat had left me with all the hated domestic chores I'd been so glad to escape. Also, as the year progressed the need for finding a job became pressing. I felt rather like a train between stations, waiting for the arrival of the call to "All change!"

But some things, particularly the bad ones, never change. You'd think that my being away from home for nigh on four years would have rendered me in the eyes of my importunate family, something of a vague, shadowy figure. No such luck! Any sort of crisis, (and these arose with depressing regularity), brought a letter, summoning me to return home and restore peace and harmony. So it was that, just when I needed to concentrate on taking my final exams, my mother, with her usual impeccable sense of timing, decided to leave home to live with a new man, leaving my two sisters shattered and heartbroken and my father alarmed and unable to cope. So, I was promptly sent for to sort out the crisis.

My feelings on the subject ranged from fury to helplessness. We were not just allowed to go home when it pleased us: we had to ask for permission. Anyway, I had no inkling what I could possibly do to remedy what seemed to be an intractable problem. I could hardly drag my mother back by her hair to fulfil her wifely and motherly duties, could I? But neither could I just abandon college and stay home to take her place and comfort my shocked and bewildered sisters. However reluctantly, however, I had to do something, so I asked Professor Sykes for permission to go home for the weekend. I don't suppose I told him the real reason why I had to go: the sordid details of my family's imminent disintegration were not things I wanted people to know, but, permission granted, I took the bus home. Home: the usual chaos, untidy rooms, no food in the house, utter disorder and my sisters inconsolable and tearful. My father seemed powerless to do anything, so it was left to me to dry the girls' tears, get in some decent food and promise to return soon, before catching the bus back to Leicester and another world.

Back in Leicester I had to put to one side the picture of my sisters' suffering, (the younger one was barely 12), and get on with the pressing task of getting a degree. I immersed myself in the old routine of essays, work in the library and the other minutiae of living, and was immensely cheered to receive some time later a letter from my father saying that my runaway mother had returned home. He didn't say what had prompted this unexpected solution to my problem, but I was glad of the tremulous stability that was returned to the household while I was otherwise engaged. It wasn't to last, of course, but at least it gave me a breathing space, a precious few weeks when I could prepare for my final exams.

Exams! The very word went through the students like a dose of salts. Even the most desultory suddenly found themselves spending long hours, nose in books, in the library, hoping that even death-bed repentance would be enough to ensure salvation, come the dreaded day of reckoning. Word went round among the overwrought of the sad fate of some students in other departments, who had had nervous breakdowns and been dragged off to languish in mental hospitals, but the more sanguine dismissed the tales as being exaggerations. When, however, Professor Sykes smugly observed that his students were made of sterner stuff and never had such extreme reactions to exam stress, we merely grimaced weakly and wondered just how close we had come to being the feeble wimps he so despised!

However, exams came and went, as they are wont to do. We went mechanically from room to room, answering questions, filling page after page of what we hoped was deathless prose, pushed by an inexorable desire to get them over with. People turned up at the wrong time, in the wrong place, even on the wrong day, and one person even overslept for an afternoon exam, but all too soon came the time for us to read our fate, in stark black and white, on a sheet of paper pinned up on the noticeboard for all to see. To our intense relief we'd all passed and although there were those who felt affronted that their obvious brilliance had not found sufficient recognition in the class of their degree, we were, for the most part, pleased with our performance. Actually, since there were only 19 of us, and our progress was so minutely charted by Professor Sykes, the quality of our brains had already been assessed and the exams were merely confirmation of what was already known about our talents.

All that remained now was for us to have our degrees conferred upon us officially in the grand setting of the De Montfort Hall. It struck me as being an entirely appropriate setting for the final act of our years at Leicester, since the Hall gave out onto Victoria Park, which had seen so many of our comings and goings during our years at university. To my astonishment, my mother, no doubt feeling that it was incumbent upon her to show maternal pride at such a moment, informed me that both she and my brother would attend the degree ceremony, the time for which was rapidly approaching.

So it was that on the appointed day we prayed for fine weather, so that we could parade afterwards in the park in our academic dress, showing off what it had taken us four long years to earn. We'd already ordered our black gowns, three-cornered caps and hoods of regal scarlet and silver - all we needed was the time to come for us to wear them.

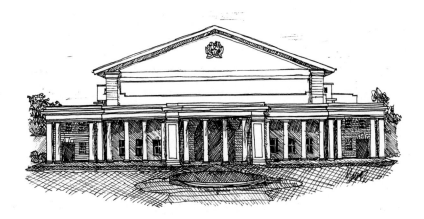

The De Montfort Hall

Dressed in sober 'academic dress' - white blouse and black skirt for the girls, dark suit and white shirt for the boys - we went to collect our hired finery and tried it on: long gowns, like yards of blackout material saved from the war, and which billowed out in the breeze as we walked, giving us an aura of Count Dracula on a gala day; the splendid hood that had to be anchored by a tape to a button on the front of the blouse, lest it slip down behind and half throttle you; finally, the black hat, oddly-shaped and which had to be securely attached to the hair by a veritable forest of pins, for fear that it might slip off at some vital point in the proceedings and reduce the solemn occasion to farce.

Once ready, awkward and self-conscious in our unaccustomed dress, like actors at the first dress rehearsal, we filed into the body of the hall, looked down on from the balcony by our proud relations and waited for the ceremony to begin. At the appointed time, the organ began and everyone rose for the academic procession. What a sight it was! Preceded by a liveried flunkey carrying the university mace, came the long procession of staff, clad in gowns and hoods of every colour.

Men robed in purple, scarlet, blue, wore huge floppy black hats of sensual velvet which made them look for all the world like ancient portraits of medieval scholars. Hoods of every hue: dark brown, emerald, with pink fur, velvet stripes, braiding, all the colours of numerous university faculties. It was a truly impressive sight, which really gave us the feeling of being part of an age-old tradition of academic achievement and excellence, of being some of the priveleged ones, chosen to carry on the tradition of scholarship.

As the Dean of our faculty called out our names, we went up on stage individually (not in batches like a bulk order, as students are obliged to do now, because of sheer numbers) and the Chancellor, the venerable Lord Adrian, intoned a few words of impressive if unintelligible Latin over our bent heads, whereupon we crossed the stage and went down the steps the other side. We were not, in those early days, given certificates to prove our new status. It was considered that our word would be enough to persuade prospective employers of our qualifications. Actually, my prospective employer didn't take my word for it and I was obliged to write to the university for confirmation of my status.

But, sad to say, even in 1962 times were on the change. Bob Dylan's "The times, they are a-changing" was sadly prophetic, for when I went back to Leicester, a mere 7 years later, to receive my M.A. degree, the magic had gone. I suppose I should have been prepared for it: the last few years had seen rebellion astir. Buildings were sat in, lectures boycotted, protest marches were organised and civil disobedience became the order of the day. The local newspaper, "The Leicester Mercury" reported in an exasperated tone that "the students seem too warlike and organised to fit into the pattern of the downtrodden they pretend to be", and this ought to have prepared me for what was going to happen. But it didn't. We were sitting quietly in the hall, the ceremony was proceeding in the time-honoured fashion, with the Chancellor conferring degrees, when, suddenly, the platform was invaded by a brigade of what looked like the army of the great unwashed: a dirty, hairy, grubby-jeaned tribe, whose leader, as hairy as Lenny the Lion, seized the microphone and denounced in somewhat incoherent if vehement terms, the university, the political system and a whole range of societal values and traditions. This done, they each took the certificates they had just received (for by this time the university had been forced to issue certificates to its ever-growing band of graduates), and tore them up ostentatiously, sprinkling them like confetti from the stage onto the heads of the astonished and furious graduates in the first two rows of the audience. Then, protest made, they made a noisy, shuffling exit, to go and lie about in untidy heaps on the grass in the park, like piles of rubbish awaiting collection. The rest of us, enraged that our big day had been so carelessly and needlessly ruined, took our certificates, gave back our hired robes and went home, thoroughly deflated. University life, we knew then, would never be the same again. Before long, the cosy, human universities would become huge, monolithic structures, catering for thousands of students, like monstrous sausage factories which produce not people but student numbers. What we'd just witnessed was the death of a system where academic rigour and intellectual training and discipline would give way to market forces and economic necessity, and I, for one, was sad.